Back to *Basics*

Woodworker's Guide to

Turning

Back to *Basics*

Woodworker's Guide to

Turning

*Straight Talk for Today's **Woodworker***

skills institute press

Distributed By
Fox Chapel Publishing

FOX CHAPEL
PUBLISHING

© 2010 by Skills Institute Press LLC
"Back to Basics" series trademark of Skills Institute Press
Published and distributed in North America by Fox Chapel Publishing Company, Inc.

Woodworker's Guide to Turning is an original work, first published in 2010.

Portions of text and art previously published by and reproduced under license with Direct Holdings
Americas Inc.

ISBN 978-1-56523-498-7

Publisher's Cataloging-in-Publication Data

    Woodworker's guide to turning : straight talk for today's woodworker.
-- East Petersburg, PA : Skills Institute Press ; published and
distributed in North America by Fox Chapel Publishing, c2010.
      p. ; cm.
      (Back to basics)
      ISBN: 978-1-56523-498-7
      Includes index.

      1. Turning (Lathe work)--Technique. 2. Spindles (Machinetools)--
Technique. 3. Woodworking tools--Maintenance and repair.
4.Woodwork--Patterns. I. Title. II. Series: Back to basics (Skills
Institute Press)

TT202 .W663 2010
684/.083--dc22 1011

To learn more about the other great books from Fox Chapel Publishing, or to find a retailer near you,
call toll-free 800-457-9112 or visit us at www.FoxChapelPublishing.com.

Note to Authors: We are always looking for talented authors to write new books
in our area of woodworking, design, and related crafts. Please send a brief letter
describing your idea to Acquisition Editor, 1970 Broad Street, East Petersburg, PA 17520.

Printed in China
First Printing: November 2010

Contents

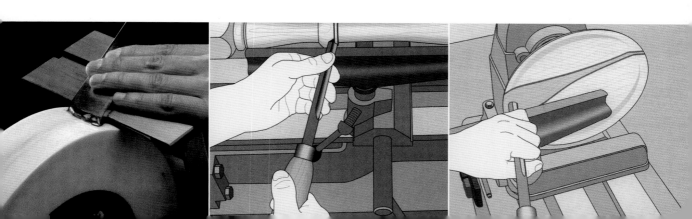

What You Can Learn

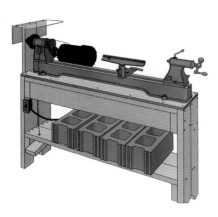

Setting Up, page 14

This chapter is an introduction to the lathe and the tools and accessories needed for turning wood blanks into furniture parts, bowls, and other finished products.

Sharpening, page 34

Dull cutting edges are not only more difficult and dangerous to use, but will also produce poor results, so take the necessary few minutes to sharpen your tools before you turn on the lathe.

Spindle Turning, page 48

Spindle turning involves mounting a wood blank between the machine's headstock and tailstock and using a variety of turning tools to shape furniture parts such as chair legs and bedposts.

Faceplate Turning, page 84

Faceplate turning produces bowls and plates. It offers the wood turner a great deal of design freedom and completes a project in one single process.

Turning Projects, page 118

Spindles and bowls are only two of the seemingly endless variety of objects that can be turned, including goblets, table tops, and lidded boxes.

The Basics of Turning Wood

As an industrial arts student at the University of Missouri many years ago, I first used the lathe to spindle turn the pedestal for a table. Since then, my techniques and knowledge have grown and matured—as has the field of wood turning itself. While I still enjoy making traditional spindle-turned furniture and objects, I also like what I see others accomplishing. Multi-centered and sculptural turnings have pushed back the frontiers of what can be created on the lathe.

As with any craft, wood turning demands a strong foundation in the basics: the properties of wood, tools and techniques, and design considerations. Building on this knowledge gives you the ability to express your creativity in a host of challenging ways, from the traditional to the avant-garde.

Spindle turning represents one of the basics that a wood turner should master. Among other things, it improves tool control, which helps with faceplate turning as well. As a professional, full-time wood turner, I structure my teaching around the basics; it gives people a place to start, and it helps me to continue learning in the process. From the Indianapolis Children's Museum to WoodenBoat School in Maine to the Ontario Wood Show in Canada, I have derived tremendous satisfaction from watching young and old getting hooked on turning. One of my goals as editor of *American Woodturner* is to provide readers with knowledge of the basics and to entice them with examples of what they could accomplish.

The growing interest in turning is focused primarily on making bowls; new ideas of what bowls and vessels should look like abound. I, too, am fascinated with faceplate turning, as it holds potential for development in years to come. Much of my faceplate work is not functional; the pieces are simply lovely to behold.

As I continue to explore the vast arena of wood turning, I have become more and more aware of the complexity and diversity of the craft. The field is wide open, ready to be explored, and I am happy to be immersed in an exciting and rewarding career.

- *Betty Scarpino*

Betty Scarpino operates a wood turning studio out of her home in Indianapolis, Indiana. As editor of *American Woodturner,* Scarpino travels throughout the United States and Canada teaching and demonstrating her wood turning expertise.

The Art of Wood Turning

Wood turning has come of age. Recent years have seen a tremendous increase in the number of people interested in the craft—from hobbyists turning in their basement shop to professionals making a living with their lathes.

Wood turning as an art form began in the 1940s with the likes of Bob Stocksdale, Melvin Lindquist, Rude Osolnik, and James Prestini. Although working independently, they were pursuing the same goals: refined and elegant turned wood objects, whether functional or purely decorative. The 1970s and early '80s saw a new generation of turners willing to push the boundaries of what was esthetically acceptable and technically possible: Mark Lindquist turning spalted wood and using chain saws to produce sculptural objects; David Ellworth pioneering the use of bent tools to produce thin-walled hollow turnings with incredibly small openings; Bill Hunter carving and sculpting the outside of vessels after the piece was turned.

The American Association of Woodturners, now 15,000 members strong, was formed in 1985. These days, an annual symposium of the AAW provides easy access to information and instruction for anyone interested in the subject. Workshops around the country, as well as books and video tapes, also fulfill the same role.

I have been supporting myself and my family as a full-time wood turner for many years, selling my work through galleries and craft shows, and teaching wood turning throughout the United States and several other countries. Although I teach bowl turning, the work that I do is primarily hollow-turned vessels featuring carved and textured surfaces. They are turned from green wood, with the grain oriented parallel to the axis of the lathe, also known as spindle turning. This provides more stability as the wood dries. I am always after the perfect curve, the fine line, the subtle details.

There are many valid approaches and ways to turn wood, and I would like to offer just three basic rules to help aspiring turners:

1. SHARP TOOLS: Not only are sharp tools much more effective, they make turning a lot more fun! A large percentage of the problems you experience will be directly caused by tools that are not as sharp as they should be.

2. TURN: There is no substitute for time on the lathe. Experience counts.

3. HAVE FUN!—Don't be so serious that you can't enjoy the process. Turn just for the joy of turning, improving your skills and making shavings, knowing that you don't have to produce a finished product every time you turn.

- John Jordan

John Jordan is a professional wood turner from Antioch (Nashville), Tennessee. He has produced several videos on wood turning, and his works are on display in several museums and corporations.

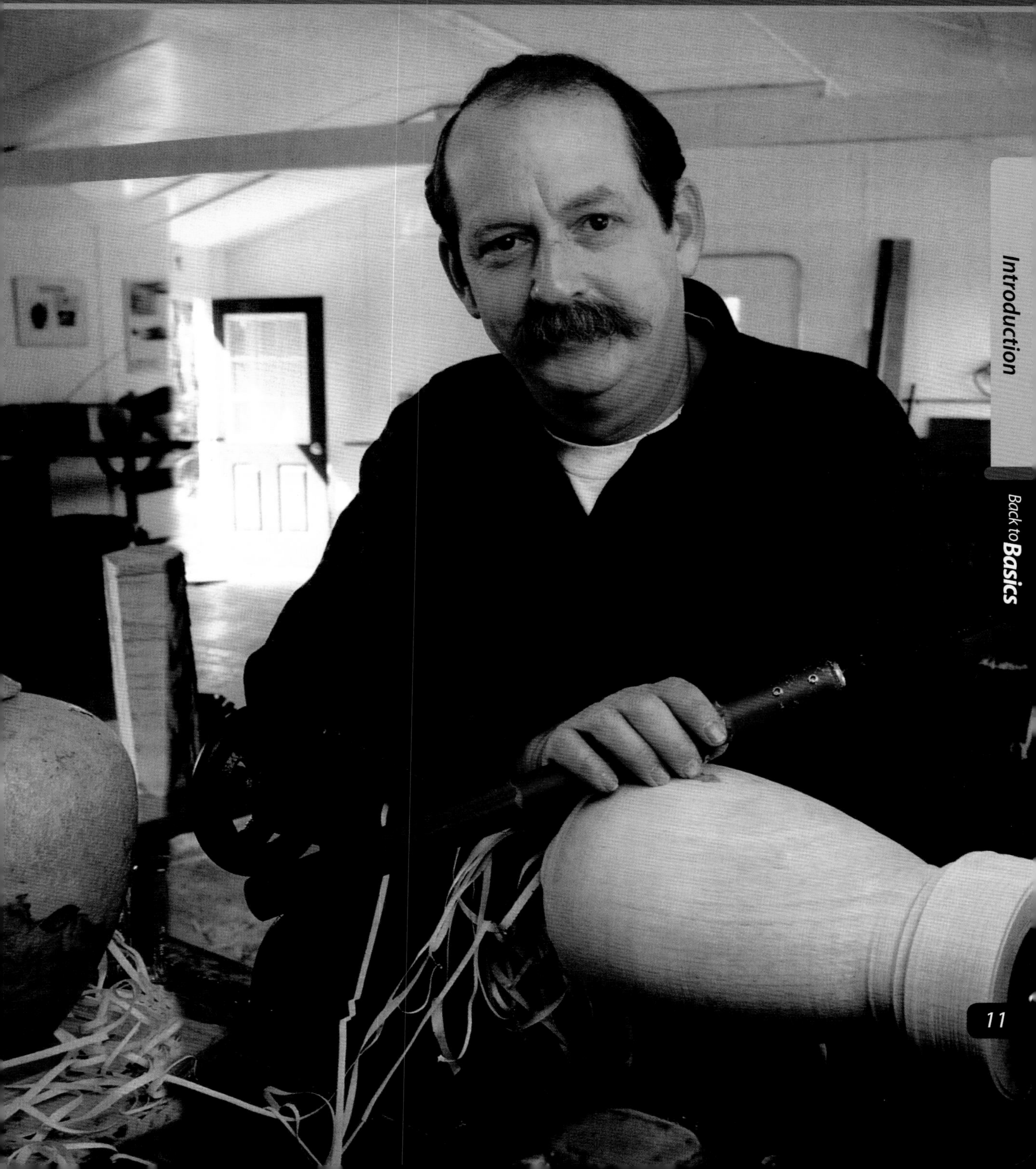

The Appeal of Wood Turning

I turn simply for the love of the creative process. I am addicted to discovery, progress, and the fact that while perfection is forever elusive, yesterday's challenges often become the basic skills of tomorrow. I love the distinct smell of the various woods, the sound of shavings as they are cut by a sharp tool, and the quickness with which a form emerges from a block of material.

In the past I have enjoyed many other crafts, such as spinning, weaving, and basketry. Each offers its own appeal to the senses: the aroma of spinning fresh wool, the sound of a shuttle, the smell of wet reeds for a basket, and the clicking of knitting needles. Experimenting with turning unusual materials such as bone, plastic, tagua nuts, aluminum, and horn has led to many more interesting sensations for eyes, ears, hands, and nose.

I have been making things for as far back as I can remember, but when I discovered wood turning it became my favorite way to create something. It started when my daughter wanted a doll house. During the process of building, lighting, and furnishing the house, I became interested in the small-scale tools I needed to use. Maybe that fascination came from the fact that my father was once a builder himself.

Several years ago, I designed and began producing a small wood turning lathe, like the one shown in the photograph. My machine has a 5-inch swing and is 12 inches between centers. A wide range of accessories is available including chucks, tools, a threaded jig, and an indexing plate. This was a new beginning for what I like to call "small-scale turning," and what has developed into an area of its own in the wood turning world, with tools, classes, projects, and even gallery shows.

One of the great virtues of a small lathe is its portability. Many people now take a lathe with them to use at craft fairs, on vacation, or south for the winter. I am able to travel with 10 lathes, tools, and wood in the back of my van to teach classes. There are many school districts that have purchased several small lathes and the necessary tools—all for the price of a large lathe. Shop teachers especially like the quietness of the machine and the fact that many of the small-scale projects may be turned from scraps.

Because wood turning is something I feel strongly about, I have volunteered many hours of teaching turning to kids. I am involved with turning full time and I feel very fortunate that I am able to earn a good income from selling lathes, tools, turnings, and my expertise.

- Bonnie Klein

Bonnie Klein is a wood turner in Renton, Washington. She is featured here turning a spinning top—one of her favorite small-scale production items—on the Klein lathe, which she developed in 1985.

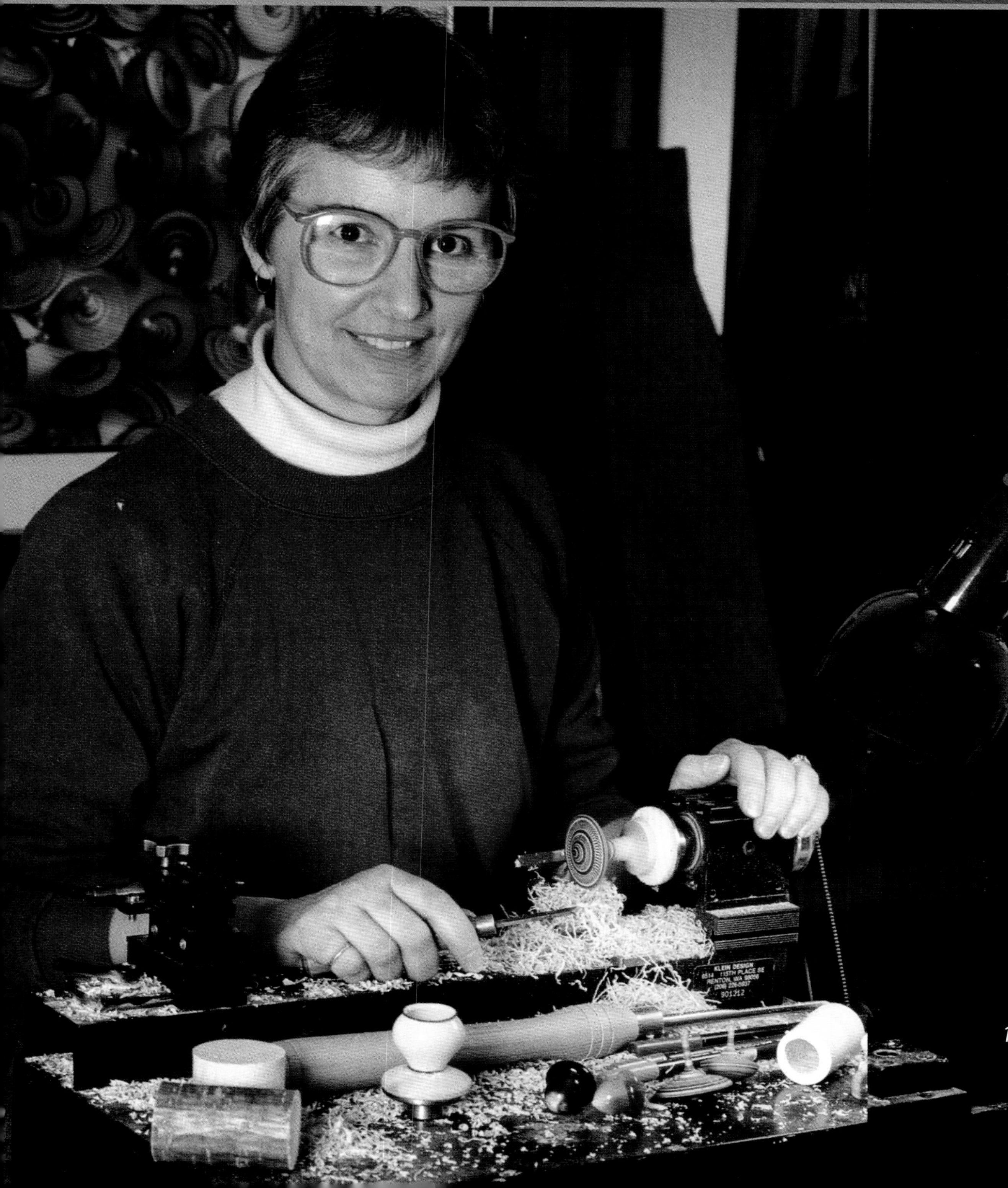
KLEIN DESIGN

Setting Up

The wood lathe is perhaps the oldest of all woodworking machines. Primitive forms of this tool were used by the Etruscans in the 9th Century B.C. And throughout its long history, the tool has been used in virtually the same way. Somewhat like a potter's wheel laid on its side, the lathe spins a wood blank while a turner shapes the wood with chisel-like tools. The lathe makes it possible to shape wood into flowing, rounded forms in a way that other tools cannot.

The earliest lathes were human-powered, with a piece of cord wrapped around the blank, connected to a springy sapling and a treadle. With a few modifications, this evolved into the pole lathe popular with British bodgers, who traveled from town to town, working freshly fallen trees into chairs. Flywheels and driveshafts were added to the design, and the lathe emerged as one of the engines behind the mass production of Windsor chairs in the mid-18th Century. Turning became a specialized trade.

With the coming of the Industrial Revolution, heavy-cast engine-powered lathes forever took the elbow grease out of turning. With minor changes, these lathes were essentially the same as those used by modern woodworkers *(page 16)*. Indeed, many wood turners prefer older lathes to newer ones, refurbishing them and setting them on stands of their own making *(page 20)*. Woodworkers were

beneficiaries of technological advances in machining made during the Industrial Revolution when lathes were adapted to turn metals, as well as wood. This new field brought the wood turner a wide range of chucks and accessories to hold the most delicate and tricky of turned objects, from goblets to lace bobbins.

The chapter that follows is an introduction to the lathe and the tools *(page 22)* and accessories *(page 25)* needed for turning wood blanks into furniture parts, bowls, and other finished products. Also included in the chapter is a section on safety precautions and equipment *(page 30)*.

The lathe remains one of the most popular woodworking tools, and wood turning is a craft with an intriguing cachet, like carving or marquetry. It is not hard to understand why: A lathe enables the woodworker to turn something beautiful from nothing more than a stick of wood.

Turning blanks are typically available in short pieces. Some of the more popular examples are shown in the photo above. Resting atop a zebrawood board are samples of tulipwood, kingwood, and ebony. For a selection of the best woods for turning, refer to page 33.

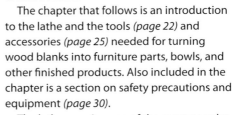

Turned legs and other furniture parts are shaped on the lathe in a process called spindle turning. In the photo at left, a wood blank is mounted between the lathe's fixed headstock in the upper left-hand corner and the adjustable tailstock near the center of the photo. The tailstock can slide along the lathe bed to accommodate the workpiece. The blank will be turned into a cylinder and then shaped with a variety of turning tools.

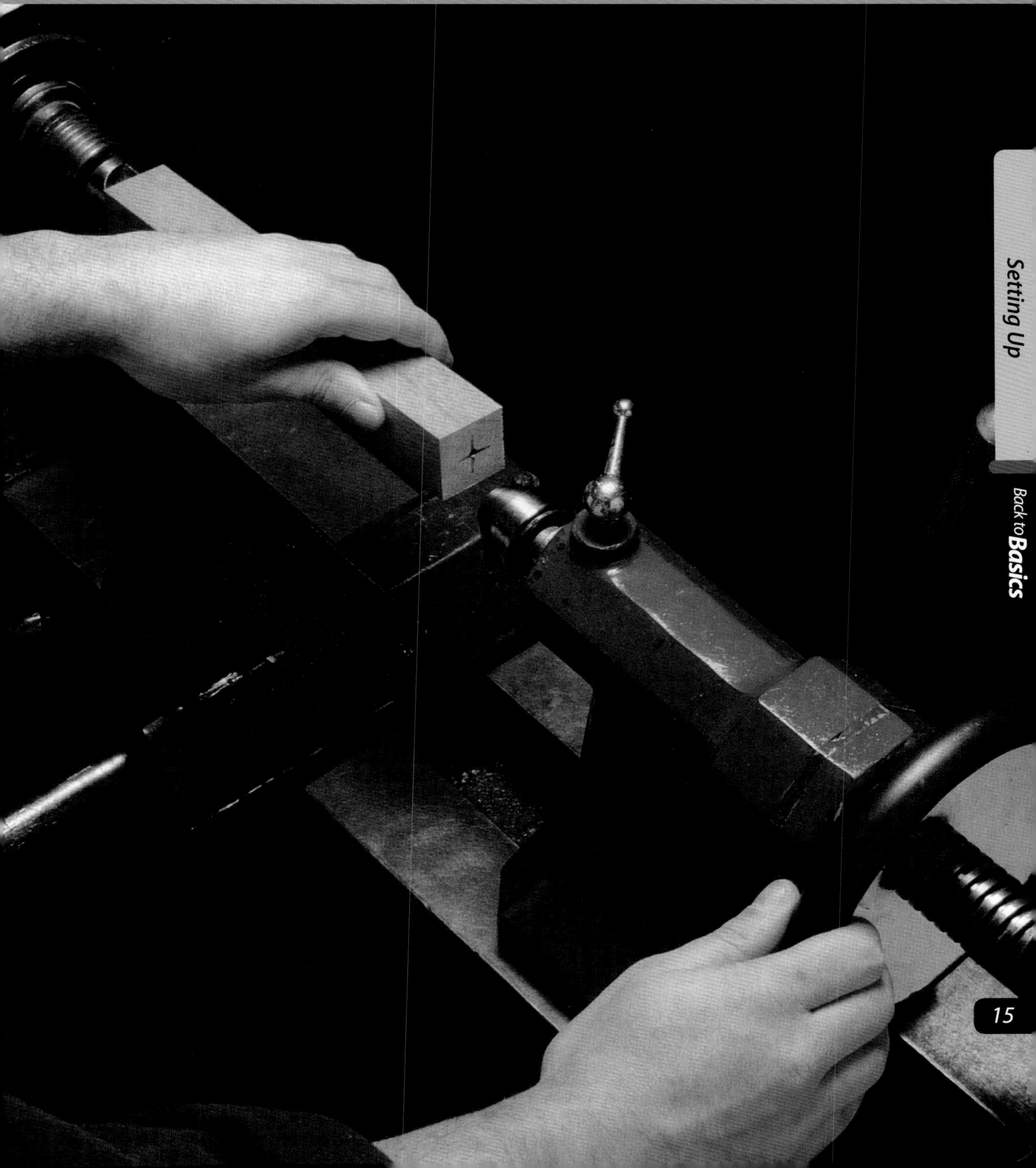

Anatomy of a Lathe

When you choose a lathe, consider carefully the type of turning you will be doing. Some models are made specifically for faceplate turning, in which the blank is secured only on the head-stock. Others are small enough to rest on a benchtop. The lathe shown below is a typical freestanding model used for both spindle and faceplate turning.

Lathe size is measured in two ways: swing and capacity. Swing is twice the distance between the headstock spindle and the bed, which limits the diameter of blanks. Capacity is the distance between the headstock and tailstock, which limits the length of blanks. The weight of the lathe is important, as greater weight provides stability and dampens vibration. Another feature to consider is

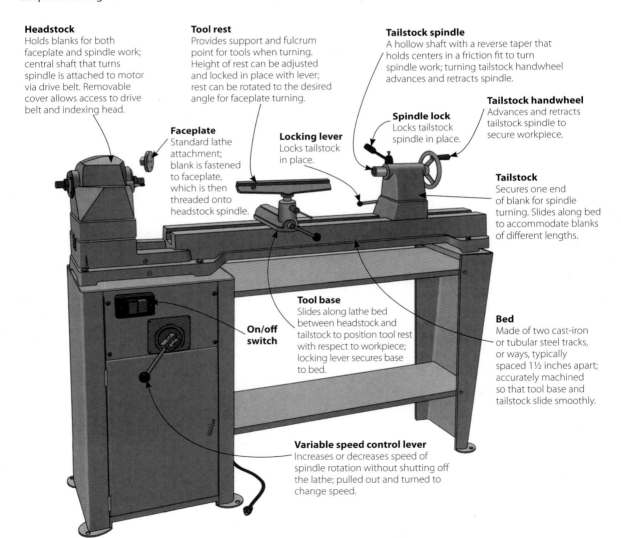

Headstock
Holds blanks for both faceplate and spindle work; central shaft that turns spindle is attached to motor via drive belt. Removable cover allows access to drive belt and indexing head.

Tool rest
Provides support and fulcrum point for tools when turning. Height of rest can be adjusted and locked in place with lever; rest can be rotated to the desired angle for faceplate turning.

Tailstock spindle
A hollow shaft with a reverse taper that holds centers in a friction fit to turn spindle work; turning tailstock handwheel advances and retracts spindle.

Tailstock handwheel
Advances and retracts tailstock spindle to secure workpiece.

Spindle lock
Locks tailstock spindle in place.

Faceplate
Standard lathe attachment; blank is fastened to faceplate, which is then threaded onto headstock spindle.

Locking lever
Locks tailstock in place.

Tailstock
Secures one end of blank for spindle turning. Slides along bed to accommodate blanks of different lengths.

Tool base
Slides along lathe bed between headstock and tailstock to position tool rest with respect to workpiece; locking lever secures base to bed.

On/off switch

Bed
Made of two cast-iron or tubular steel tracks, or ways, typically spaced 1½ inches apart; accurately machined so that tool base and tailstock slide smoothly.

Variable speed control lever
Increases or decreases speed of spindle rotation without shutting off the lathe; pulled out and turned to change speed.

how easy it is to change speeds; larger workpieces must be turned at lower speeds than smaller ones. Changing the speed of some lathes involves switching a drive belt between two sets of stepped pulleys; other models have variable-speed pulley systems that allow the speed to be changed without switching off the tool.

If you decide to buy a used lathe, check the motor, bearings, spindle threads, and lathe bed for wear. Make sure the tool rest and tailstock run smoothly and all locking levers work. Also make sure that the spindle thread is standard; if not, chucks and other accessories must be rethreaded to fit.

Headstock Assembly

Fixed-width pulley
Features four adjustable steps. On lathes with variable-speed adjustment, spindle speed is changed by manually moving belt from one step to another; on variable-speed models, belt is left as is.

Indexing head
Enables spindle to be rotated a preset number of degrees by hand when carving flutes, reeds, and spiral turnings on a blank. Features one ring of 60 holes spaced 6° apart around the head and another of 8 holes spaced 45° apart; indexing pin is inserted in a hole when carving is being done and taken out to rotate spindle. Lathe must be switched off during entire operation.

Spindle nut
Loosens to remove spindle for replacing belts and bearings.

Headstock spindle
Threaded hollow shaft to which various chucks are screwed in place; ranges from ½ inch to 1½ inches in diameter. Hollow is Morse-tapered to hold various centers with a friction fit.

Indexing pin
Fits into holes in indexing head; inserted to hold headstock spindle steady and retracted to rotate spindle by hand.

Drive Assembly

Variable-speed pulley mechanism
Can be adjusted to set lathe to different spindle speeds while lathe is running.

Drive belt

Motor

Motor bracket
Holds motor in position to ensure correct belt tension; loosened to replace belts or change speed on the fixed-width pulley.

The 1950s-vintage Wadkin Bursgreen lathe is prized for its machining capacities and innovative features, such as a brake that stops spinning blanks quickly and a removable bed segment near the headstock to accommodate large-diameter faceplate work.

Tool Rests and Lathe Stands

A tool rest acts as a fulcrum for your turning tools, providing a fixed, horizontal weight-bearing surface for balancing and bracing a tool as you cut into a spinning blank. The tool rest on a lathe is made up of two parts: a tool base and the detachable rest itself. The base can slide along the length of the lathe bed, according to the needs of the work. The tool rest mounts in the base; the height and angle of the rest are adjustable so it can be positioned parallel to the lathe bed for spindle and faceplate work, perpendicular to the bed for faceplate work, or at an angle in between. In addition, the base and rest can be mounted on an outboard bed for large-diameter faceplate turning. There are a number of different tool rests for specialized turning tasks; a selection is shown below.

Shop Tip

Weighing down a lathe
Because turning wood can cause a great deal of vibration, a lathe needs to be as stable as possible. Even the best lathe is an inefficient and dangerous machine if it is not weighed down properly. Because most modern lathe stands are made of lightweight steel, it is necessary to weigh them down with cement blocks or sacks filled with sand, as shown here, to reduce vibration and noise. Bolting the lathe to your workshop floor is another option.

Tool Rests

Standard tool base
Slides along the lathe bed; features a fitting for tool rest shaft. A lever-operated cam mechanism locks base in position on the bed. Base shown is the type that comes with most lathes.

Standard tool rest
Mounts in tool base for general faceplate and spindle work; comes with lathe.

S-shaped bowl rest
Used for turning the outside and inside of bowls.

Tall tool base
Used on lathes with lower outboard beds for turning large faceplate work, this base is 4 inches taller than standard bases; a lever-operated cam mechanism is used to lock the base in position.

Short rest
Used for smaller spindle and faceplate work; typically 6 inches long.

Right-angle rest
Mounted in standard tool rest to turn bowl blanks; long side is positioned perpendicular to lathe bed to turn face of bowl, while short side is positioned parallel to lathe bed to work sides. Long side typically measures 7 inches.

Long rest
Mounted in two standard tool bases for long spindle work; available in 18- and 24-inch lengths.

Dressing a Tool Rest

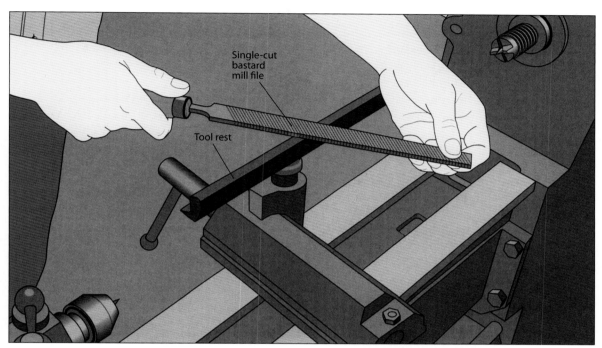

Single-cut
bastard
mill file

Tool rest

Smoothing a worn tool rest

Because a tool rest is made of softer steel than the steel used for turning tools, it will eventually develop low spots, marks, and nicks. If not remedied, these imperfections will be transferred to the blanks you turn, or make the tool you are holding skip and possibly cause an accident. You can dress a tool rest easily with a single-cut bastard mill file. Holding the file in both hands at an angle to the rest, push it across the top surface *(above)*. Make a series of overlapping strokes until you remove all the nicks and hollows from the rest, then smooth the surface with 200-grit sandpaper or emery cloth followed by a light application of floor wax, buffed smooth.

Shop Tip

Adjusting lathe height

The height of a lathe is crucial to efficient turning. Commercial lathe stands are often too low, which can make it difficult to control your turning tools. You also may tire more as a result. As a rule of thumb, the height of a lathe's spindles should be level with your elbows. If necessary, you can raise your lathe to the proper height by bolting it to solid blocks of dense hardwood with foam rubber glued to their undersides.

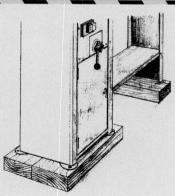

A Lathe Stand

Older lathes are prized by wood turners because they were often built better than newer models. The only problem is that these vintage lathes often lack a stand or a working motor. Fortunately, it is easy to equip a lathe with both. Lathes need less powerful motors than most stationary machines. A ½-hp model that runs at 1725 RPM—half the speed of a table saw motor—will do.

A lathe stand needs to be heavy and solid, like the rugged shop-built version shown below, constructed primarily from 2-by-6s. The motor is mounted behind the lathe, with the pulleys under a safety guard.

The stand also features a wooden tension pedal that allows you to release belt tension and stop the spindle instantly. Refer to the illustration for suggested dimensions.

For the stand, start by cutting the legs to length from four 2-by-6s, then saw a triangular notch from the bottom of each leg to make feet. Join each pair of legs with two crosspieces, locating one crosspiece just above the feet and the other 1½ inches from the top of the legs. Cut the shelf from two 2-by-6s, and screw the pieces to the lower leg crosspieces.

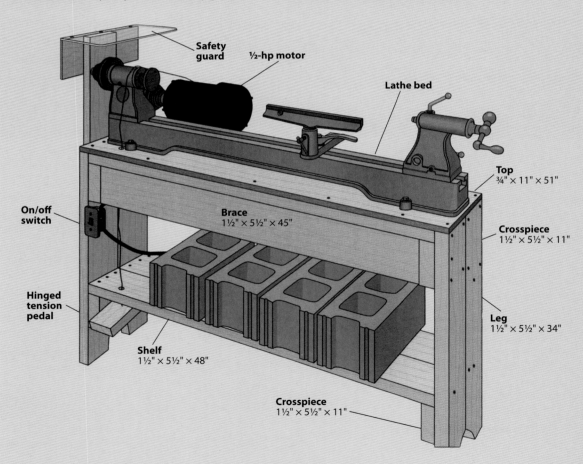

Safety guard

½-hp motor

Lathe bed

Top
¾" × 11" × 51"

On/off switch

Brace
1½" × 5½" × 45"

Crosspiece
1½" × 5½" × 11"

Hinged tension pedal

Leg
1½" × 5½" × 34"

Shelf
1½" × 5½" × 48"

Crosspiece
1½" × 5½" × 11"

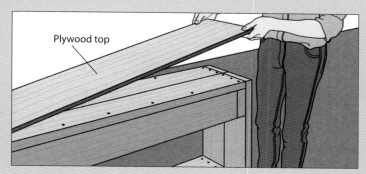

Plywood top

Next, install the top, cut from two 2-by-6s and a piece of ¾-inch plywood. Screw the boards and two braces to the upper leg crosspieces, then fasten the plywood to the 2-by-6s, as shown above. Bolt the lathe to the top of the stand.

Screw the motor to a mounting board cut from ¾-inch plywood. Then fasten the board to the top with butt hinges so the steps in the motor pulley are in line with the headstock pulley steps (below). Mount the drive belt on the pulleys.

Next, make and install the tension pedal. Connected by a length of wire to the motor-mounting plate, this wooden pedal will allow you to slacken the drive belt with simple foot pressure, disengaging the motor from the headstock and stopping spindle rotation. Cut the pedal from 2-by-4 stock so that it will extend out from under the shelf by about 4 inches when it is installed. Attach the tension pedal with another hinge to the underside of the shelf, directly under the motor. Bore holes through the top, the shelf, and the pedal to accommodate the wire that will connect the pedal to the motor-mounting board. Attach a length of heavy-gauge wire to the underside of the pedal and pass it through the three holes you drilled and over the headstock. Now push the motor-mounting board toward the lathe and hold the wire against it. Keeping the tension pedal flat on the floor, pull the wire taut. Cut the wire and screw it to the back of the motor mounting board (below). Release the motor; the tension pedal should rise from the floor. To check the pedal, step on it; the wire should pull the motor-mounting board and motor towards the lathe, releasing the tension on the belt.

Lastly, install an on/off switch for the motor at the front of the lathe stand, and place concrete blocks or other heavy objects on the shelf to weigh down the stand and reduce vibration.

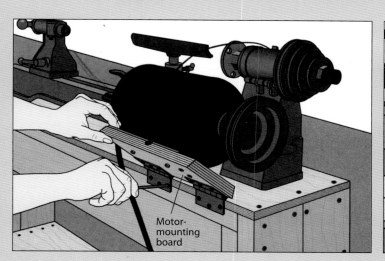

Motor-
mounting
board

Heavy-
gauge
wire

Hinged
tension
pedal

Setting Up

Back to **Basics**

21

Lathe Tools

Unlike other stationary machines, the lathe is not equipped with blades or bits. Instead, you need to buy a set of turning tools to do your work. These tools resemble wood chisels, except they are tempered and shaped differently, with longer handles and blades for better control and leverage.

Turning tools can be divided into two basic groups: cutting and scraping tools. Cutting tools are most often used in spindle turning, where the grain of the wood runs parallel to the lathe's axis of rotation. These tools include gouges, chisels, and parting tools. Scraping tools are usually used in faceplate turning, where the grain runs perpendicular to the axis of rotation.

Traditionally, all turning tools were made of carbon steel, but this material has a tendency to overheat during grinding and with continuous use. Turning tools made of high-speed steel (HSS) retain their edge up to six times longer than carbon steel, making the additional expense worth it in the long run. In fact, some tools, like deep-fluted bowl gouges and large scrapers, are only

Cutting Tools

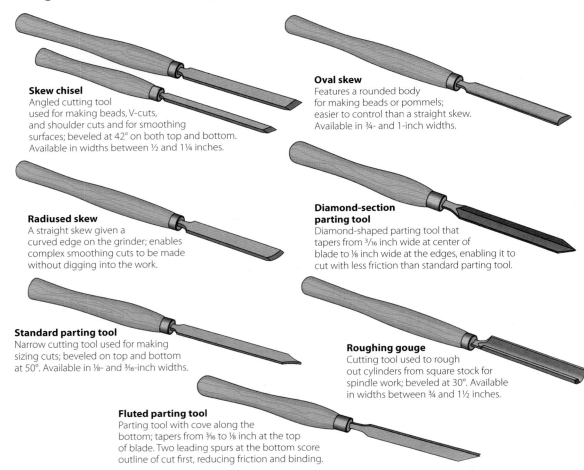

Skew chisel
Angled cutting tool used for making beads, V-cuts, and shoulder cuts and for smoothing surfaces; beveled at 42° on both top and bottom. Available in widths between ½ and 1¼ inches.

Oval skew
Features a rounded body for making beads or pommels; easier to control than a straight skew. Available in ¾- and 1-inch widths.

Radiused skew
A straight skew given a curved edge on the grinder; enables complex smoothing cuts to be made without digging into the work.

Diamond-section parting tool
Diamond-shaped parting tool that tapers from ³/₁₆ inch wide at center of blade to ⅛ inch wide at the edges, enabling it to cut with less friction than standard parting tool.

Standard parting tool
Narrow cutting tool used for making sizing cuts; beveled on top and bottom at 50°. Available in ⅛- and ³/₁₆-inch widths.

Roughing gouge
Cutting tool used to rough out cylinders from square stock for spindle work; beveled at 30°. Available in widths between ¾ and 1½ inches.

Fluted parting tool
Parting tool with cove along the bottom; tapers from ³/₁₆ to ⅛ inch at the top of blade. Two leading spurs at the bottom score outline of cut first, reducing friction and binding.

available in HSS. Whether they are made from high-speed or carbon steel, turning tools should always be kept sharp, using techniques described in the following chapter beginning on page 34. A blunt tool is an accident waiting to happen.

There is a bewildering variety of turning tools on the market, yet only eight to 10 are needed to undertake most common turning. A beginner's tool kit is outlined below, at right.

In their quest for better tools, some wood turners design their own. California engineer and wood turner Jerry Glaser developed a line of turning tools using A-11 high-speed steel, some of which are shown in the photo at right. The hollow aluminum handles are filled with lead shot to dampen vibration and give the proper weight to the tool. Some of the handles and blades are interchangeable.

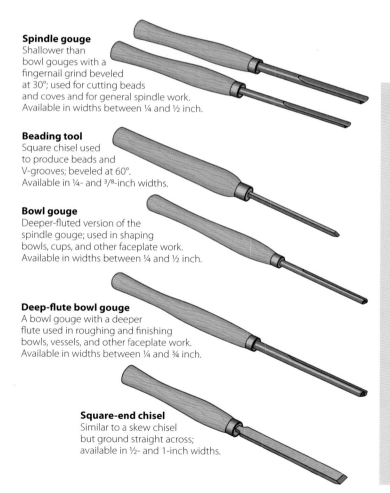

Spindle gouge
Shallower than bowl gouges with a fingernail grind beveled at 30°; used for cutting beads and coves and for general spindle work. Available in widths between ¼ and ½ inch.

Beading tool
Square chisel used to produce beads and V-grooves; beveled at 60°. Available in ¼- and ³⁄₈-inch widths.

Bowl gouge
Deeper-fluted version of the spindle gouge; used in shaping bowls, cups, and other faceplate work. Available in widths between ¼ and ½ inch.

Deep-flute bowl gouge
A bowl gouge with a deeper flute used in roughing and finishing bowls, vessels, and other faceplate work. Available in widths between ¼ and ¾ inch.

Square-end chisel
Similar to a skew chisel but ground straight across; available in ½- and 1-inch widths.

A Wood Turner's Basic Tool Kit

- A *1-inch roughing gouge* for rapid removal of stock between centers

- *2 skew chisels*: a ¾- or 1-inch tool for planing and tapering, and a ½-inch tool for finer work, such as shaping curves and making decorative cuts

- *2 spindle gouges*: a ¾- or 1-inch tool for general spindle turning, and a ½-inch tool for finer spindle work

- A *¼-inch diamond section parting tool* for parting off and making sizing cuts

- A *³⁄₈-inch bowl gouge* for faceplate turning of bowls up to 10 inches in diameter

- A *¼-inch deep flute bowl gouge* for faceplate turning

- A *¾-inch round nose scraper* for cleaning up concave surfaces and hollow faceplate work

- A *1-inch square-end scraper* for flattening and smoothing convex surfaces

23

Scraping Tools

Square-end scraper
Used for flattening and smoothing convex faceplate work such as the outside of bowls; cutting edge beveled on the underside at 80°. Available in widths between ¼ and 1 inch.

Side-cutting scrapers
Specialized ¾-inch scrapers used on the inside of bowls and other hollow faceplate work.

Skew scrapers
Angled 1½-inch square-end scraper for rounding convex surfaces and marking concentric cuts in faceplate work; comes in left- and right-handed models.

Round-nose scraper
General-purpose scraping tool for smoothing and finishing concave surfaces in faceplate work such as bowls or hollow vessels; available in widths from ½ to 1 inch.

Half-round scraper
Larger 1½-inch version of round-nose scraper for heavy-duty bowl work; comes in left-and right-handed models.

Domed scraper
Version of round-nose scraper for making fine shearing cuts and finishing inside of bowls and other hollow faceplate work; available in widths between ½ to 1 inch.

Specialty Tools

Hook tool
Patterned after specialty Swedish wood-turning tools; used in end-grain hollowing. Short hook is for hollow work with gradual interior curves; long hook is for forms with tight internal curves, such as a necked vase. Sold without handles.

Disk chisel
Features a 1-inch beveled disk at tip; tip is removable for sharpening.

Ring tool
Used for end-grain hollowing of vases, boxes, and other hollow turnings; ideal for areas difficult to reach with a bowl gouge. Interchangeable cutting rings are sharpened on the inside bevel; removed and installed with a setscrew. Rings are ⁵⁄₁₆, ⁷⁄₁₆, and ⁹⁄₁₆ inch in diameter.

Lathe Accessories

Mounting stock in a lathe requires several basic accessories. If you are turning between centers, or spindle turning, you will need a variety of centers that fit in the headstock and tailstock of the machine *(page 26)*. These centers grip the blank at both ends as it turns.

Faceplate turnings, such as bowls or plates, can be screwed to a simple faceplate and threaded onto the headstock. Smaller or more delicate turnings, such as lace bobbins, should be held by a chuck.

There is a wide range of lathe chucks, each serving a different purpose, from the simple screw chuck to the scroll chuck. The latter comes from the field of metalwork and features three or four jaws that open or close around the workpiece. Some chucks are designed as combination chucks, and comprise a number of parts that can be reconfigured to hold stock in several ways.

Bowls can be mounted for finishing their bases with a set of wide jaws, an accessory for a four-jaw scroll chuck. The jaws hold the bowl rim with rubber stoppers that are screwed into a series of holes. Some models have adjustable slots in addition to the holes so the jaws can hold irregularly shaped faceplate work; the model shown can be used with bowls up to 10 inches in diameter.

A Collection of Chucks

Arbor screw chuck
Used to mount faceplate work to the headstock; mounts in pilot hole drilled in workpiece. Includes a 2½-inch backing washer for large work; some models feature adjustable screws.

Spigot chuck
Used to mount faceplate work to the headstock; chuck collar tightens spigot jaw around either dovetail or parallel spigots turned in the base of workpiece. Part of combination chuck system.

Jacobs chuck
Three-jaw chuck used to hold small turning work in the headstock or boring attachments in the tailstock; features Morse taper shaft.

Three-way split ring chuck
Used to mount long hollow turnings such as goblets and vases to the headstock; beveled rings fit into sizing cut made in workpiece and lock against beveled internal face of chuck collar. Part of combination chuck system.

Dovetail chuck
Used to mount bowls and other faceplate work to the headstock; as screw collar is tightened with wrenches shown, beveled jaws expand against a dovetailed recess turned in base of workpiece. Part of combination chuck system.

Pin chuck
Used when roughing out large faceplate blanks mounted to the headstock; inserted into hole bored in workpiece. Part of combination chuck system.

Four-jaw scroll chuck
Another combination chuck system that can be used as a dovetail, spigot, pin, or screw chuck; jaws expand and contract on slides as chuck scroll is rotated with wrenches shown. Larger jaws can be added.

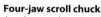

Threading accessory
Lathe jig used to turn external and internal threads in faceplate workpieces. Turned workpiece with chuck or faceplate is mounted in jig which is then installed on lathe bed; cutter and Jacobs chuck are mounted in headstock. Work is then advanced into cutter by turning handwheel to cut threads.

A Selection of Centers

Two-spur drive center
Mounted in headstock spindle to center and drive spindle work; point centers the workpiece while chisel-like spurs engage and turn it. Features Morse taper shaft; useful with blanks whose ends are not square.

Four-spur drive center
Mounted in headstock spindle to center and drive spindle work; features Morse taper shaft. Offers better grip and drive on square-cut work than two-spur center.

Cone center
Used with a live center to support hollow workpieces that are held at the headstock end only; cone has several steps of decreasing diameters.

Dead center
Mounted in tailstock spindle to center and drive spindle work; features Morse taper shaft. Remains fixed with respect to spinning work; some lubrication is needed. Model shown is a cup center, featuring raised ring to prevent splitting of small work.

Lace-bobbin center
Mounted in headstock to turn small work such as bobbins; features Morse taper shaft. Tapered square hole will hold stock ⁵⁄₁₆- to ½-inch square.

Live center
Mounted in tailstock spindle to center workpiece; features Morse taper shaft. Large hub contains bearings, allowing center to spin with the work, eliminating friction.

Shop Tip

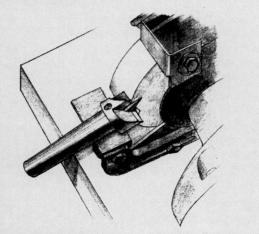

Sharpening a drive center
Drive centers should be kept as sharp as your turning tools. If the spurs or point of a drive center are dull or chipped, they will not grip the workpiece properly between centers, resulting in an off-center mounting. To sharpen a drive center, grind a 35° bevel on the underside of each spur on a bench grinder, as shown here. Do not keep the spurs on the wheel too long, as the heat generated may soften them. Then remove the centerpoint with a hex key and sharpen it to a uniform taper. Replace the point in the center so that it protrudes ⅛ inch beyond the spurs, and tighten it with the key.

Two Racks for Turning Tools

Keep your turning tools organized and within reach with one of these shop-built racks. They are simple to make; adapt the dimensions in the illustrations to accommodate your tool collection. The rack shown at top is made from ¼- and ¾-inch plywood; it features spacers to separate the tools and a brace that prevents them from falling forward. To make the rack, cut the back, top, bottom, and sides of the frame and screw the pieces together. Mount the spacers to the back with a screw at the top and bottom, spacing the strips every 2½ inches. Finally, position the brace about 1 inch from the bottom of the rack and screw it to every second spacer.

The rack shown at bottom relies on a magnetic bar to hold tools upright. Instead of a frame, this rack features a ¾-inch plywood backing panel. Cut the lip from solid wood and bore a row of 2-inch-diameter holes to accommodate the handles of your turning tools; drill each hole halfway through the lip and space them 2½ inches apart. Attach the lip flush with the bottom of the panel, driving screws from the back. To position the magnetic bar, set a few of your tools upright in the rack—including the shortest one—and mark a line across the panel at the level of the blades. Screw a 1-inch-square strip of wood to the panel over the line and glue a magnetic strip to the wood with contact cement.

As a safety consideration, whichever rack you build, mount it beside—not behind—your lathe. This will eliminate having to reach over the tool while it is running.

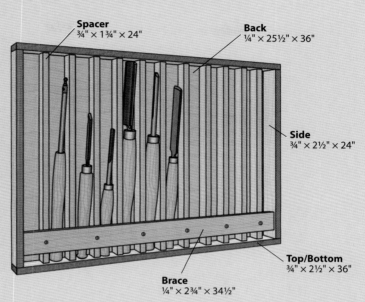

Spacer
¾" × 1¾" × 24"

Back
¼" × 25½" × 36"

Side
¾" × 2½" × 24"

Top/Bottom
¾" × 2½" × 36"

Brace
¼" × 2¾" × 34½"

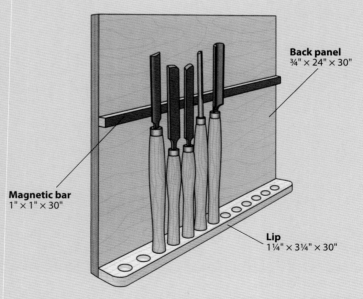

Back panel
¾" × 24" × 30"

Magnetic bar
1" × 1" × 30"

Lip
1¼" × 3¼" × 30"

Setting Up

Back to **Basics**

27

Measuring and Marking Tools

Despite its visual appeal and emphasis on "feel" as a method of judging the progress of a workpiece, wood turning is an exacting craft. To obtain the required precision, the headstock of your machine must run smoothly and true, and the workpiece must be carefully centered.

The tools illustrated below and on page 29 will help you to set up your lathe and accurately measure the progress of your work. Use them well; it is difficult to judge a bowl's depth by eye or duplicate the contours of a turned leg without a set of calipers.

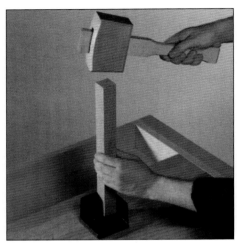

The commercial center finder shown in the photo at right takes the guesswork out of mounting spindle stock to the lathe. The jig is particularly useful for round and octagonal stock, and for remounting work once the waste ends have been cut away. The blank is held in the bottom of the jig, rapped with a mallet, rotated a quarter turn, and then hit again. The two lines scored on the end will indicate the center of the piece. For added convenience, mount the jig on a wall.

Checking the Bearings for Runout

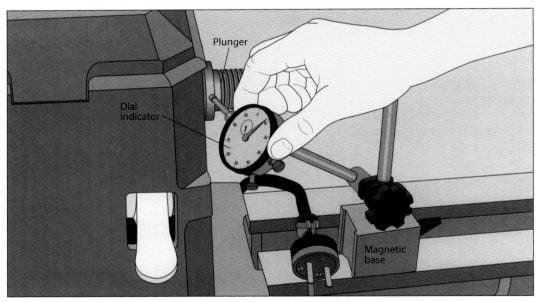

Plunger

Dial indicator

Magnetic base

Using a dial indicator

If your lathe is an older model, check the bearings periodically for runout—the amount of wobble in the spindle. Clamp a dial indicator to a magnetic base and position it with its plunger touching the lathe's spindle *(above)*, then calibrate the dial to zero following the manufacturer's instructions. Turn the shaft of the lathe by hand; the dial indicator will register bearing runout. If the runout exceeds 0.005 inch, the bearings should be replaced.

Measuring and Marking Tools for Wood Turning

Combination calipers
Feature a set of inside calipers at one end and a set of outside calipers at the other; useful for sizing lids to fit turned boxes. Available in 6- to 12-inch spans.

Inside calipers
Used to determine inside diameter of hollow turnings; available in 4-, 6-, and 8-inch spans.

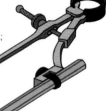

Outside calipers
Used to determine thickness of spindle or faceplate work; available in 4-, 6-, and 8-inch spans.

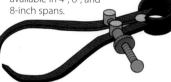

Dial calipers
Usually used to measure wall thickness; makes precise inside and outside measurements. Graduated in $\frac{1}{1000}$-inch increments.

Compass
Used to scribe a circle on a blank; typical span is 6 to 8 inches.

Double-ended calipers
Feature a set of outside calipers at each end. A dimension taken at one end is automatically transferred to the other; calipers do not have to be removed from workpiece to take measurement. Available in 8- and 10-inch spans.

Center finder
Quickly locates center of square, round, or octagonal spindle stock up to 6 inches wide; features steel scoring blade to mark stock.

Depth gauge
A shop-made gauge consisting of a wood handle and two dowels used to determine the depth of bowls and hollow turnings; the longer dowel features depth increments. Model shown can measure bowls up to 17 inches in diameter.

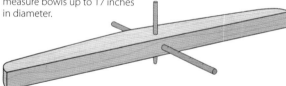

Sizing tool
Attached to a beading or parting tool, as shown, for producing accurate diameters in spindle work; knob opposite cutting edge rests against spinning blank as cutter reduces thickness.

Setting Up

Back to Basics

29

Safety

Although turning is considered to be a relatively safe pursuit, it is not free of danger. Getting your fingers pinched between a spinning blank and a tool rest is only one hazard. Most turning accidents can be attributed to mounting a blank on the lathe improperly, or using inappropriate speed or tool technique. Carefully center a blank on the spindle and check that you are using the proper speed for the job before you start turning. The speed must be compatible with the size and weight of the workpiece. Finally, never use a cutting tool for something it was not designed to do, and make sure your tools are sharp.

The safety accessories shown below are as important as sharp tools. Because of the large amount of chips and dust produced by turning, eye and face protection are essential. Wood dust packs some hidden hazards as well. Exotic woods, such as rosewood and tulipwood, produce toxic dust that can cause serious eye, throat, and skin irritation. Wear a dust mask or respirator when turning any wood and equip your shop with an adequate dust collection system. A shop-made dust hood for the lathe is shown on page 31.

Safety Accessories for Turning

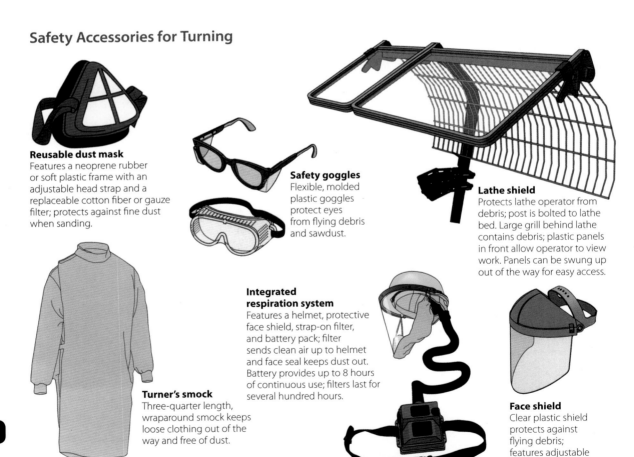

Reusable dust mask
Features a neoprene rubber or soft plastic frame with an adjustable head strap and a replaceable cotton fiber or gauze filter; protects against fine dust when sanding.

Safety goggles
Flexible, molded plastic goggles protect eyes from flying debris and sawdust.

Lathe shield
Protects lathe operator from debris; post is bolted to lathe bed. Large grill behind lathe contains debris; plastic panels in front allow operator to view work. Panels can be swung up out of the way for easy access.

Integrated respiration system
Features a helmet, protective face shield, strap-on filter, and battery pack; filter sends clean air up to helmet and face seal keeps dust out. Battery provides up to 8 hours of continuous use; filters last for several hundred hours.

Turner's smock
Three-quarter length, wraparound smock keeps loose clothing out of the way and free of dust.

Face shield
Clear plastic shield protects against flying debris; features adjustable headband.

A Dust Hood for the Lathe

Turning can generate a great volume of waste wood and dust. Built entirely from ¾-inch plywood, the dust hood shown at right can be positioned directly behind a workpiece to draw chips, shavings, and sawdust from your lathe and convey this debris to your dust collector. Refer to the illustration for suggested dimensions. Make the stand high enough for the hood to sit at the level of the workpiece when the base is on the shop floor.

To build the jig, cut the base and stand, and connect them with an edge half-lap joint. Next, cut the four sides of the hood, starting with 12-inch-square pieces and tapering each to 6 inches at the back. Use glue and screws to connect the pieces. Cut a panel to fit the opening at the back of the hood, beveling its edges so that it fits snugly. Use a saber saw to cut a hole for a dust collection hose, then glue and screw the back panel to the hood. Attach the hood to the stand with three angle brackets on each side of the stand. The front of the hood should protrude over the edge of the stand to balance the assembly.

To use the jig, insert a dust collector hose into the back panel. Place the dust hood directly behind the workpiece and turn on the dust collector before you start turning. You can install casters at the bottom of the base and stand, if desired.

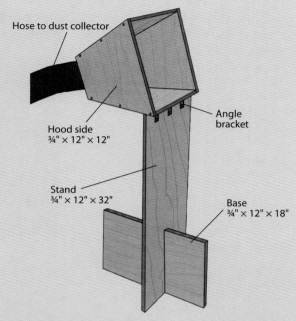

Hose to dust collector

Angle bracket

Hood side
¾" × 12" × 12"

Stand
¾" × 12" × 32"

Base
¾" × 12" × 18"

Turning Safety Tips

- Do not wear loose clothes, neckties, or rings while turning; remember to roll up your sleeves.

- Wear appropriate safety equipment at all times.

- Make sure the lathe is properly grounded, and on its own electrical circuit.

- When finishing, do not use large cloths, as they may catch and pull your fingers into the work.

- Check the speed of your lathe before you turn it on; do not use excessive speeds.

- Ensure there is adequate lighting for your work. The lathe should have as much natural light as possible; place it by a window if your shop has one.

- When using the indexing pin, make sure the lathe is unplugged to prevent the spindle from rotating accidentally; be sure to disengage the pin before plugging in the lathe.

- Check for defects in the wood you are planning to turn; avoid blanks that have twists, splits, or knots.

- Always use the correct tool for the job.

- While turning, concentrate on the work at hand, and take frequent breaks to avoid fatigue.

- Always work with tools that are properly sharpened. Dull tools are more dangerous than sharp ones

- Keep the tool rest as close to the workpiece as possible without interfering with your ability to use your tools properly; rotate the work by hand first to see that it turns freely.

- Do not operate the lathe under the influence of alcohol or medication.

Changing the Lathe Speed

Loosening the drive belt

To change the speed on a lathe that features stepped pulleys, unplug the machine and lift open the headstock cover. Step on the tension lever to disengage the ratchet and raise the motor, releasing the drive belt tension and loosening the belt *(right)*.

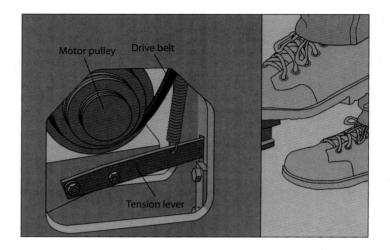

Motor pulley   Drive belt

Tension lever

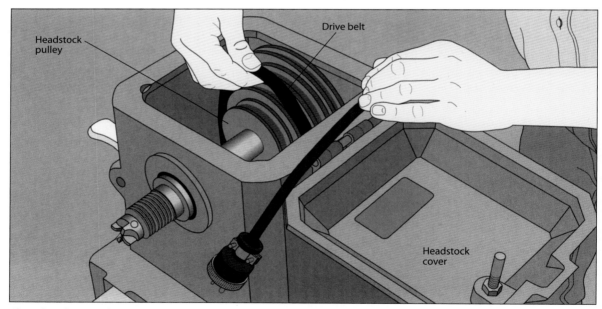

Headstock pulley

Drive belt

Headstock cover

Changing the speed

To set the desired speed, follow the manufacturer's instructions for adjusting the position of the belt. (On the model shown, these instructions are printed on a nameplate on the underside of the headstock cover.) Position the drive belt on the appropriate step on the motor pulley and then align it with the correct step on the headstock pulley *(above)*. Once the drive belt is in position, step on the tension lever again to lower the motor and tighten the belt. Close the headstock cover.

Selecting Wood

In some ways, selecting wood for turning is like choosing lumber for any woodworking project. Stock should be free from defects, such as knots, splits, checks, and shakes. Blanks for spindle turning should be straight-grained; for bowls and other faceplate work, grain is less of a concern. In fact, a wildly figured piece of wood can yield a stunning bowl.

In other ways, selecting wood for turning has some advantages: Since wood turners are not limited to boards and planks, small offcuts at the lumber-yard or fallen fruit trees at a local orchard can provide the needed raw materials.

Turning is typically done with hardwoods, as softwoods are often incapable of rendering sharp detail.

Exotic woods are popular with many turners because of their striking figure; however, many are being harvested at an alarming rate, and some are scarce and very expensive. Check with your local dealer for exotics from well-managed sources. See the list below for the characteristics and uses of some common turning woods.

While it is preferable to turn wood that has been air-dried or kiln-dried to a moisture content of 8 to 10 percent, green wood can sometimes be used. Blanks for large, deep bowls are sometimes best cut from a freshly felled tree. Yet while green wood is easier to turn, it shrinks more, and end sealer should be used to help prevent excessive checking.

A Selection of Woods for Turning

Wood Type	Characteristics and Uses	Price and Availability
Apple	Hard, tough wood with attractive straight grain and fine, even texture; light sapwood, reddish-brownish heartwood. Good workability; accepts finishes well. Excellent for small, ornate turnings.	Moderate; relatively plentiful
Cocobolo	A heavy, dense tropical exotic with medium texture and straight to irregular grain; purple, orange, rust and yellow in color with black markings. Moderate workability; finishes well and takes a high polish yet produces noxious dust when sanded. Used for small spindle turning projects such as vases, cutlery and tool handles.	Expensive; scarce
Mahogany	Straight to interlocked grain, moderately coarse texture, light reddish-brown to medium red. Good to excellent workability, depending on species; takes finishes very well; a tough, strong wood for general turning.	Moderate; becoming scarce
Maple	Straight grain, occasionally curly or bird's-eye, fine texture; reddish-brown heartwood and white sapwood. Good to moderate workability; accepts finishes very well. Hard and dense, maple is suitable for general and fine turning.	Inexpensive to moderate, depending on figure; relatively plentiful
Olivewood	Interlocked grain with fine, even texture; yellowish-brown with variegated streaks. Moderate to difficult workability; accepts finishes very well and takes an unusually high polish. Ideal for ornate turning.	Expensive; rare
Pear	Straight grain; fine, even texture; pinkish-brown to reddish-brown. Excellent workability; takes a high polish. Typically used for fine, ornate turning, and musical instruments.	Expensive; rare
Rosewood	Straight to interlocked grain, depending on the species; golden-brown to dark, purple brown. Good workability; accepts finishes well, provided the species is not too oily. Used for fine turning.	Expensive; becoming scarce
Tulipwood	Irregular grain, medium-fine texture; rich golden-pinkish hue with salmon to red stripes. Difficult workability; splits easily. Accepts finishes very well; can be brought to an unusually high polish, yet produces noxious dust when sanded. Used for small, ornate turnings.	Very expensive; scarce

Sharpening

Sharp tools are the cornerstone of wood turning. Dull cutting edges are not only more difficult and dangerous to use, they will also produce poor results. Take the necessary few minutes to sharpen your tools before you turn on your lathe.

The first step of sharpening involves grinding a tool's bevel to a suitable angle. There is some disagreement among turners as to what this angle should be for every tool. But as long as a bevel is either hollow-ground (concave) or flat, it will work well. As you gain experience, you may settle upon angles that suit your style of turning. Grinding is discussed on page 36.

Not surprisingly, there are several ways to sharpen turning tools. A few turners do all their sharpening with benchstones and slipstones. Others sharpen exclusively on a grinding wheel. This is a quick and easy method of forming the edge you need, particularly midway through a turning project when you want to touch up an edge quickly. A wheel, however, may leave rough marks on the blade, preventing it from cutting cleanly and causing it to dull relatively quickly. As shown in this chapter, there is a good compromise: Start by rough-sharpening at the grinder and finish by honing the edge on a benchstone or slipstone. A bench grinder's felt wheel will perform the job of a slipstone, polishing the bevel to a razor-sharp edge (page 40). Scrapers differ from cutting tools in that they depend on a burr instead of an edge for cutting. The burr can be made with a grinder, a bench stone, or a burnisher (page 47).

Once you have chosen a sharpening method, you will need to develop a technique. Seasoned turners sharpen freehand, but for the beginner, a commercial sharpening jig for use on a grinder is a worthwhile investment. There is a wide range of sharpening stones and wheels available. The inventory on page 36 and the chart of grinding wheels on page 38 should provide you with the information you need to make an informed purchase.

Like turning tools, grinders themselves require maintenance. Dressing the wheel occasionally (page 38) will ensure that your tools are being sharpened by fresh abrasive particles. Check your wheels for cracks by tapping them: A wheel in good condition will produce a ringing sound. As an additional safety precaution, wear eye protection whenever you grind.

The secret to raising a burr on a scraper—an essential step in the sharpening process—is to apply light pressure as you hold the blade against the grinding wheel.

A wet/dry grinder is valuable for sharpening turning tools. Its wheel rotates more slowly than that of a conventional bench grinder, reducing the risk that the temper of the steel will be destroyed.

Sharpening Techniques

Before you can sharpen a turning tool, the bevel angle must be ground properly. The grinding requirements of cutting and scraping tools are very different because of the way they are used on the lathe. The bevel of a cutting tool must rub on the stock at all times to help control the cut. If the angle is too sharp, the tool will be harder to control and the cutting edge will dull quickly. But if the bevel angle is too steep, you may have to hold the tool almost vertically and apply excessive pressure. Scrapers, on the other hand, shave away wood with a burr. The angles they require depend on the type of scraper you are using.

Not only bevel angle, but the shape of the tip—whether straight across, skewed at an angle, or curved—is important to consider when grinding your tools. A square-ground spindle gouge, with a tip ground perpendicular to the blade shaft, is best for turning cylinders,

tapers, or other straight cuts. A fingernail-ground spindle gouge, with edge corners cut back, or relieved, will make a better tool for turning beads and coves. Skew chisels may be ground straight across or curved, depending on the use. See page 39 for an illustration of the tips of various turning tools.

As you grind a bevel, it is critical to create a single-faceted bevel, that is, one with a continuous face. This can only be achieved by keeping the bevel perfectly flat on the wheel as you grind. The jig shown on page 41 will help you with a troublesome tool, the roughing-out gouge. If you use a grinder, the bevel will have a shallow concave shape, matching the curve of the grinding wheel. Avoid using a wheel smaller than 5 inches in diameter; the degree of curvature will make for a weak tool tip. Grinding on a belt sander *(page 43)* will yield a flat bevel, which is equally effective.

The grinder is a multipurpose tool for the wood turner. Here, the nicked cutting edge of a skew chisel is squared before grinding the bevel.

Sharpening Tools

Honing compound
Applied to cloth wheel of grinder to polish sharpened bevel; contains a mixture of chromium dioxide and other fine abrasives.

Slipstones
Small oilstones and waterstones used to hone bevels of turning tools; convex, concave, and conical stones are suited to curvatures of various gouges.

Benchstone
Any oilstone, water-stone, or diamond-stone used to hone bevel of tools.

Dresser
Used to true or reshape grinder wheels and expose a fresh cutting surface. Star-wheel dresser *(below, top)* has up to four star-shaped wheels; diamond-point dresser *(below, bottom)* features a diamond set in a bronze tip and metal shaft.

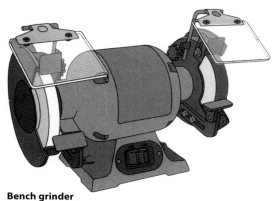

Bench grinder

Grinding or abrasive wheel *(left-hand side)* squares and sharpens blades; cloth wheel *(right-hand side)* polishes the bevel near the cutting edge. Features ¼-to ½-hp motor; eye shields, adjustable tool rests, and wheel guards are standard on most models; bench-top grinders are usually bolted to a work surface.

Multi-tool jig

Adjustable tool rest *(right)* mounts to bench in front of grinder; features a 4-inch-wide table with a slot for sliding jigs and center-drilled for rotating jigs. Skew-grinding jig *(above, top)* holds skews at 20° angle, pivots on center pin to grind radiused skews, and folds out of the way for freehand grinding. Sliding sharpening jig *(above, bottom)* clamps tools under crossbar and slides in groove in table.

Neoprene wheel

Rubber grinding/sharpening wheel; available in four grits. Used for grinding and sharpening; provides a sharp enough edge for turning without additional buffing or honing. Wheel must turn away from tool edge to prevent it from catching on the wheel surface.

Felt wheel

Available in soft, medium, or hard; dressed with buffing compound to perform final polishing of cutting edge.

Aluminum-oxide wheels

Standard grinding wheels, available in 6- and 8-inch sizes and a range of grits.

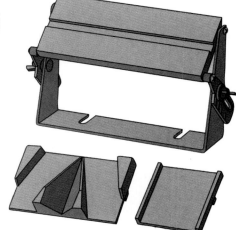

Wet/dry grinder

Large 10-inch water-bathed wheel hones bevels; water prevents tools from overheating and carries away metal and grit. Five-inch dry wheel used for grinding. Each wheel equipped with an adjustable tool rest.

Adjustable tool rest and sharpening jig

Tool rest with tilting table *(above, top)* mounts to bench in front of grinder; table has slots for sliding tool guides and four settings on side bracket to adjust table to suitable angle for bowl gouges, spindle gouges, and skews. Available with accessory tool guides for gouges and skews *(above, left)* and for straight chisels and scrapers *(above, right)*. Diamond-point wheel dresser *(right)* rides in slot in table to dress grinder wheel.

Sharpening

Back to **Basics**

Grinding Wheel Identification

Choosing a grinding wheel

The wheels supplied on grinders are usually too coarse for use with turning tools. A wide variety of replacement stones are available, but selecting the right one is no simple matter. You need to decipher the codes marked on the side of the wheels, describing their composition and abrasive quality. The chart below will help you interpret these codes. (They are usually found sandwiched between two numerical manufacturer's symbols on the side of the stone.) If you plan to use a wheel to grind carbon steel tools,

and then hone with a benchstone, buy a wheel marked A 80 H 8 V. This means the wheel is aluminum oxide (A), fine grained (80), and relatively soft (H), with a medium structure or concentration of abrasives (8). The particles are bonded together by a process of heat and fusion, known as vitrification (V). For high-speed steel tools, a medium hardness of I or J is better. If you plan to use your tools right off the grinder, choose a wheel with a grain size of 100 or 120.

Standard Marking System Chart			
Abrasive Type	**A**: Aluminum oxide	**C**: Silicon carbide	**Z**: Aluminum zirconium
Abrasive (Grain) Size	**Coarse**: 8, 10, 12, 14,16, 20, 24 **Medium**: 30, 36, 46, 54, 60	**Fine**: 70, 80, 90, 100, 120, 150, 180	**Very fine**: 220, 240, 280, 320, 400, 500, 600
Grade Scale	Soft Medium Hard A B C D E F G H I J K L M N O P Q R S T U V W X Y Z		
Structure	Dense ⟶ Open 1 2 3 4 5 6 7 8 9 10 11 12 13 14 15 16 etc		
Bond Type	**B**: Resinoid—**BF**: Resinoid reinforced—**E**: Shellac—**O**: Oxychloride—**R**: Rubber— **RF**: Rubber reinforced—**S**: Silicate—**V**: Vitrified		

Courtesy of the American National Standards Institute

Dressing a Grinding Wheel

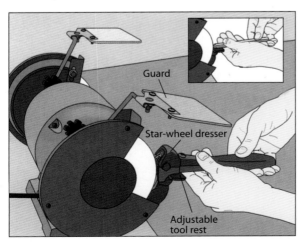

Guard

Star-wheel dresser

Adjustable tool rest

Truing the wheel

A grinding wheel should be trued when ridges or hollows appear on the stone or it becomes discolored. You can use either a star-wheel or a diamond-point dresser. For the star-wheel dresser shown at left, move the grinder's tool rest away from the wheel. With the guard in position, switch on the grinder and butt the tip of the dresser against the wheel. Then, with your index finger resting against the tool rest, move the dresser from side to side. To use the diamond-point dresser *(inset)*, hold the device between the index finger and thumb of one hand, set it on the tool rest, and advance it toward the wheel until your index finger contacts the tool rest. Slide the tip of the dresser across the wheel, pressing lightly while keeping your finger on the tool rest. For either dresser, continue until the edges of the wheel are square and you have exposed fresh abrasive.

Grinding Turning Tools

The angle at which you present a tool to the grinder will determine the angle of the bevel. The diagram at right shows the angles at which gouges, scrapers, and skew chisels should be held to the grinding wheel to produce suitable bevels.

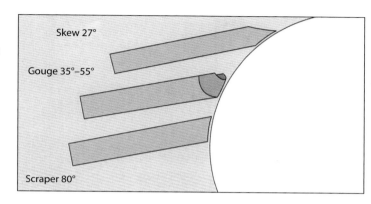

Skew 27°

Gouge 35°–55°

Scraper 80°

Turning Tool Tips

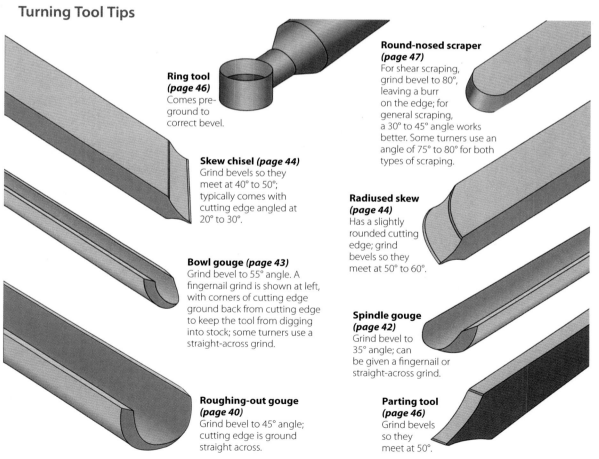

Ring tool (page 46)
Comes pre-ground to correct bevel.

Skew chisel (page 44)
Grind bevels so they meet at 40° to 50°; typically comes with cutting edge angled at 20° to 30°.

Bowl gouge (page 43)
Grind bevel to 55° angle. A fingernail grind is shown at left, with corners of cutting edge ground back from cutting edge to keep the tool from digging into stock; some turners use a straight-across grind.

Roughing-out gouge (page 40)
Grind bevel to 45° angle; cutting edge is ground straight across.

Round-nosed scraper (page 47)
For shear scraping, grind bevel to 80°, leaving a burr on the edge; for general scraping, a 30° to 45° angle works better. Some turners use an angle of 75° to 80° for both types of scraping.

Radiused skew (page 44)
Has a slightly rounded cutting edge; grind bevels so they meet at 50° to 60°.

Spindle gouge (page 42)
Grind bevel to 35° angle; can be given a fingernail or straight-across grind.

Parting tool (page 46)
Grind bevels so they meet at 50°.

Sharpening a Roughing-Out Gouge

Restoring the bevel

Position the guard and turn on the machine.
Holding the blade between the fingers and
thumb of one hand, set the cutting edge on
the tool rest and advance it until the bevel
lightly contacts the grinding wheel. If you
want to change the bevel angle of the cutting
edge, adjust the tool rest to the desired angle.
With your index finger against the tool rest,
roll the blade on the wheel until the entire
edge is ground, keeping the bevel flat on the
wheel at all times. Continue, checking the
blade regularly, until the cutting edge is sharp
and the bevel angle is correct. To prevent the
blade from overheating, occasionally dip it in
water if it is carbon steel, or remove it from
the wheel to let it cool if it is high-speed steel.
If your grinder has a felt or cloth wheel, use it
to polish the cutting edge. Otherwise, use a
slipstone *(page 42)*.

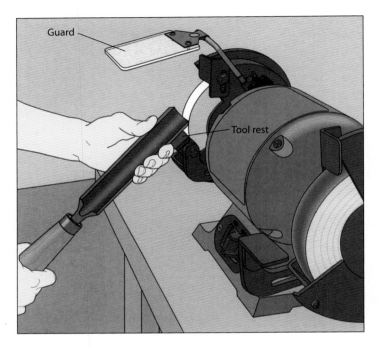

Guard

Tool rest

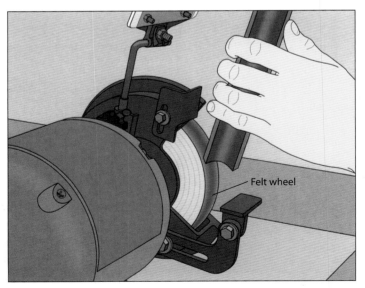

Felt wheel

Polishing the cutting edge

Move the tool rest out of the way, turn on the
grinder, and hold a stick of polishing compound
against the felt wheel for a few seconds to
impregnate it with abrasive. Then, with the
gouge almost vertical, grip the handle in your
right hand, hold the blade between the fingers
and thumb of your left hand, and set the bevel
flat against the wheel. Lightly roll the blade
from side to side across the wheel to polish the
bevel. A slight burr will form on the inside edge
of the tool. To remove it, roll the inside face of
the blade against the wheel until the burr rubs
off. Test the tool for sharpness by cutting a wood
scrap across the grain. The blade should slice
easily through the wood.

Gouge-Sharpening Jig

The jig shown at right guarantees that the tips of longer and larger gouges will contact your grinding wheel at the correct angle to restore the bevel on the cutting edge. The dimensions given in the illustration at right will accommodate most turning gouges.

Cut the base and guide from ½-inch plywood. Screw the guide together and fasten it to the base with screws countersunk from underneath. Make sure the opening created by the guide is large enough to allow the arm to slide snugly but freely.

Cut the arm from 1-by-2 stock and the tool support from ½-inch plywood. Screw the two parts of the tool support together, then fasten the bottom to the arm, flush with one end. For the V block, cut a small wood block to size and saw a 90° wedge out of one side. Glue the block to the support.

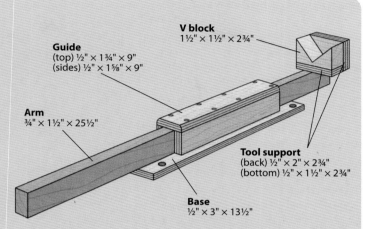

V block
1½" × 1½" × 2¾"

Guide
(top) ½" × 1¾" × 9"
(sides) ½" × 1⅝" × 9"

Arm
¾" × 1½" × 25½"

Tool support
(back) ½" × 2" × 2¾"
(bottom) ½" × 1½" × 2¾"

Base
½" × 3" × 13½"

To use the jig, secure it to a work surface so the arm lines up directly under the grinding wheel. Seat the gouge handle in the V block and slide the arm so the beveled edge of the gouge lies flat on the grinding wheel. Clamp the arm in place. Then, with the gouge clear of the wheel, switch on the grinder and reposition the tool in the jig. Holding the gouge with both hands, rotate the beveled edge across the wheel (below). Stop occasionally to cool the blade and check the cutting edge periodically until you are satisfied with the results.

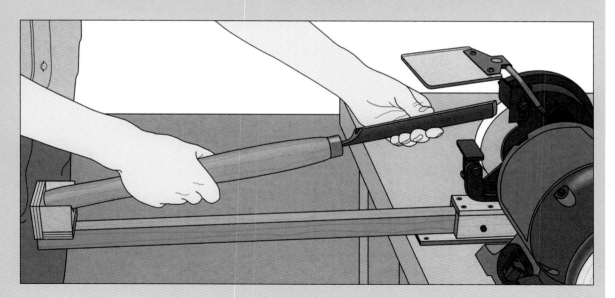

Sharpening a Spindle Gouge

Sharpening on a bench grinder

Position the guard properly and turn on the grinder. Pinching the blade between the fingers and thumb of one hand, set the blade flat on the tool rest and advance it until the bevel lightly contacts the stone *(right)*. Adjust the tool rest, if desired, to change the bevel angle. If the tool has a square grind, roll the bevel on the stone as you would for a roughing-out gouge *(page 40)*. If the tool has a fingernail-grind, roll the cutting edge on the wheel and pivot the handle from left to right while keeping the bevel flat on the grinding wheel at all times *(inset)*. Continue rolling the blade and moving the tool handle from side to side until the edge is sharpened, stopping occasionally to check the grind and cool the tip.

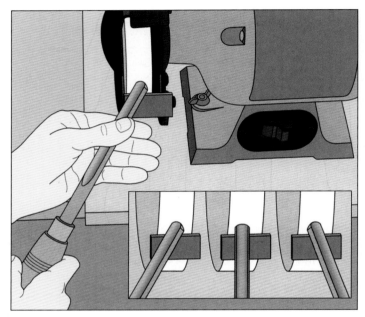

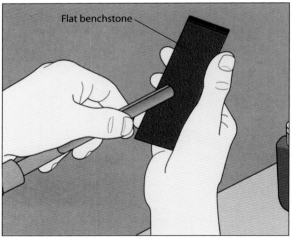

Flat benchstone

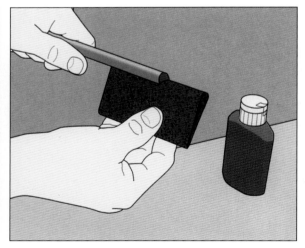

Honing the cutting edge

Once the bevel has been sharpened on the grinder, use a flat benchstone to polish the tool to a razor-sharp edge. Saturate the stone with oil, then roll the outside bevel across the abrasive surface *(above, left)* to create two microbevels on the cutting edge, as shown on page 45. Use a convex slipstone matching the curvature of the gouge to remove the burr that forms on the inside of the cutting edge. Put a few drops of oil on the slipstone and hone the inside edge until the burr rubs off *(above, right)*.

Sharpening a Bowl Gouge

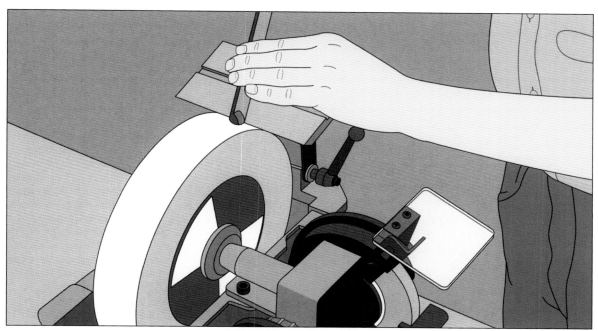

Using a wet/dry grinder

Adjust the tool rest so the bevel will rest flush with the wheel surface, then turn on the grinder. Hold the gouge flat on the tool rest and advance the tool until the bevel is flat on the stone. Then, holding the blade in place, roll the edge across the stone *(above)*, pivoting the handle as necessary to keep the bevel flat on the wheel at all times. Continue until the tool is sharp. The gouge is now ready to use.

Shop Tip

Sharpening with a belt sander

If you do not own a bench grinder, you can grind your turning tools on a belt sander. Install a 100-grit belt, mount the tool upside down in a stand, and clamp the stand to a work surface. To grind a turning tool, turn on the sander and press the bevel flat on the belt.

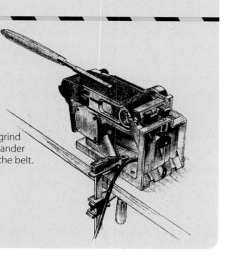

Sharpening a Skew Chisel

Using a jig
Position a commercial sharpening jig in front of the grinding wheel as close to the wheel as possible without touching it. Set up the jig following the manufacturer's instructions. On the model shown, you can adjust the tool table to the correct angle for any tool—in this case, a straight skew chisel. Place the tool guide supplied with the jig in the groove in the rest and hold the chisel in the guide. Butt one edge of the chisel blade against one side of the groove in the guide so the cutting edge is square to the grinding wheel. Turn on the grinder and advance the tool until the bevel contacts the wheel. Slide the tool guide from side to side to sharpen the bevel. Flip the tool over and repeat the process with the tool against the other edge of the groove in the guide *(right)*. When both bevels are sharpened, hone a microbevel *(page 45)*. The same techniques can be used without benefit of a sharpening jig, using the grinder's tool rest.

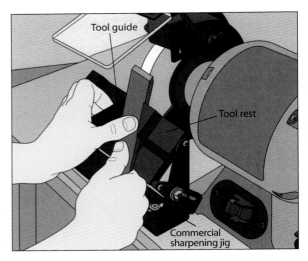

Sharpening a Radiused Skew Chisel

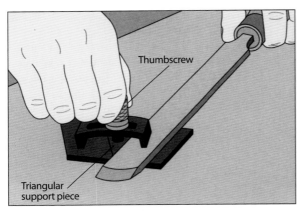

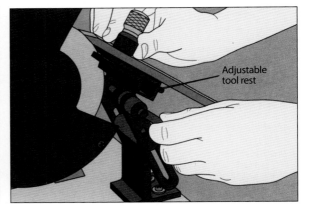

Using a radius sharpening jig
Secure the chisel in a commercial jig specially designed for sharpening radiused skew chisels. For the model shown, hold the long edge of the chisel blade against the triangular support piece in the center of the jig and tighten the thumbscrew so that the bevel will lie flat on the grinding wheel when you sharpen it *(above, left)*. Now, position an adjustable tool rest in front of the grinding wheel and set the jig on it, ensuring that the pivot pin on the bottom of the jig slides in the hole in the center of the tool rest. Adjust the angle of the rest so the bevel sits flat on the wheel, then tighten it in position *(above, right)*. Turn on the grinder and pivot the bevel across the wheel, keeping the jig pressed down on the tool rest at all times.

Sharpening the second bevel

Once the first bevel is sharpened, turn off the grinder and wrap a piece of masking tape around the chisel blade where it meets the bottom edge of the jig. This will enable you to turn the chisel over and reposition it in the jig so that the second bevel you grind is identical to the first. Remove the chisel from the jig, turn it over, and reposition it so the bottom edge of the jig is aligned with the tape. Turn on the grinder and sharpen the second bevel *(right)* the same way you ground the first.

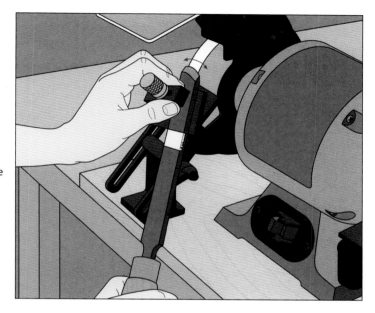

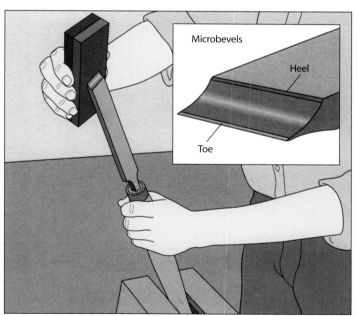

Microbevels

Heel

Toe

Creating microbevels

The grinding process will create a rough hollow-ground, or concave, bevel on the tool blade. The heel and toe of the bevel of either straight or radiused blades must be honed to a smooth cutting edge before the chisel is used. To support the chisel, wedge its handle in the lathe bed, then put a few drops of oil on the fine side of a combination stone. Rub the stone across the bevel *(left)*, creating microbevels on both the heel and toe of the bevel *(inset)*. Repeat the procedure on the other side of the tool. As the tool becomes dull with use, you do not need to regrind it. Simply restore the microbevels. After several honings, however, the microbevels will disappear and the bevel will flatten out. At this point, you will have to regrind the tool to restore the hollow-ground bevel.

Sharpening

Back to *Basics*

45

Sharpening a Parting Tool

Using a wet/dry grinder

Adjust the tool rest so the bevel on the parting tool will lie flat on the wheel. Hold the blade on edge on the tool rest with one side against the miter gauge supplied with the rest, then turn on the grinder and advance the tool until the bevel contacts the wheel. Pressing the tool lightly against the grinder, slide the gauge back and forth until the bevel is sharpened. Repeat the process to sharpen the bevel on the other side *(right)*. Once both bevels are the same and the cutting edge is sharp, hone microbevels as you would on a skew chisel *(page 45)*.

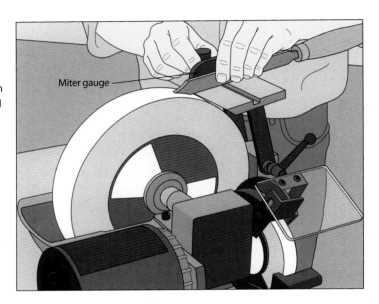

Miter gauge

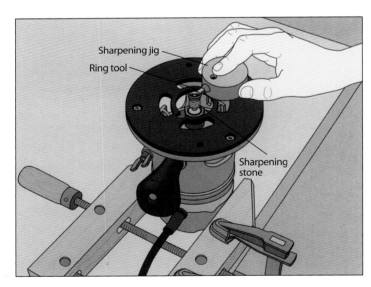

Sharpening jig
Ring tool

Sharpening stone

Sharpening a Ring Tool

Using a commercial jig

Some ring tools come with a jig for holding the tip during sharpening and a conical stone for honing the inside edge. Follow the manufacturer's instructions to sharpen your ring tool. For the model shown at right, install the sharpening stone in the collet of a router and clamp the tool upside down on a work surface. Detach the tip from the handle of the ring tool and install it in the jig. Turn on the router and press the tip lightly against the spinning stone to sharpen the edge. When the first side is sharp, flip the tool and hone the other side of the ring.

Sharpening a Scraper

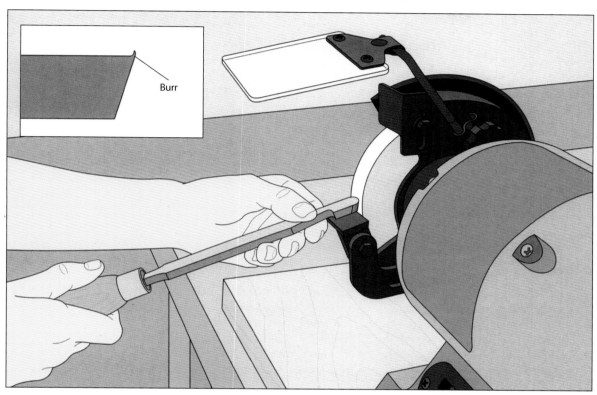

Burr

Using a grinder

Position the guard properly and adjust the tool rest so the bevel on the end of the scraper will rest flush against the wheel. Turn on the grinder and hold the blade between the fingers and thumb of one hand. With the blade flat on the tool rest, advance the tool until the bevel lightly contacts the wheel. Pass the entire edge across the wheel *(above)*, moving the handle from side to side. Stop occasionally and run your finger lightly over the end of the tool to feel for a burr *(inset)*. Stop sharpening when an even burr has formed.

Shop Tip

Burnishing a scraper
Wet grinders do not leave enough of a burr on scraper blades; you can produce a more even burr by burnishing the edge. Using firm, even pressure, draw a burnisher across the end of the blade to raise a burr on its top edge.

Spindle Turning

Of the two main activities practiced on the lathe, spindle turning is the one most closely associated with furniture making. The process involves mounting a wood blank between the machine's headstock and tailstock and using a variety of turning tools to shape furniture parts, such as chair legs and bedposts, and other decorative pieces. Because the stock is mounted "between centers, " the wood grain of the workpiece runs parallel to the axis of the lathe. In bowl or faceplate turning, which is examined in the next chapter, the grain of a blank is normally perpendicular to the machine's axis of rotation. Despite their differences, both activities do share several things in common: Correct mounting methods, proper tool use, and accurate measurement all are crucial to achieve satisfactory results.

Because spindle turning does not require cutting into end grain, the process involves relatively simple techniques, and no more than three or four tools are required. This makes turning between centers an ideal way to develop a feel for the lathe and good tool technique. On its simplest level, spindle turning is little more than connecting high and low points on a blank with shoulders, beads, and coves.

The chapter that follows is an introduction to spindle turning techniques, from the repertoire of basic spindle cuts *(page 55)* such as planing, sizing, and taper cuts to more decorative spindle cuts *(page 66)* such as beads, coves, and balls that will enhance your objects. By sawing the blank in half and regluing it, you can create symmetrical split turnings and other spindle designs *(page 75)*.

As with any activity on the lathe, the best way to learn is by experimentation. Wait until you have mastered the basic techniques before trying to reproduce complex spindle patterns. Use inexpensive wood for your blanks and practice with simple shapes until you are comfortable with the tools.

Producing a tool handle on the lathe is an ideal project for the novice wood turner. In the photo above, a Jacobs chuck in the tailstock holds a drill bit as it bores a hole for the tang at the handle-end of the blade.

Turning a well-proportioned leg requires a combination of sound technique and some creativity. In the photo at right, a spindle gouge cuts a bead near the top of the leg. Between the beads and the lathe headstock is the pommel, which is left square so that the leg can be joined to the rail of a table or chair.

A Gallery of Spindle Cuts

Spindle Cut

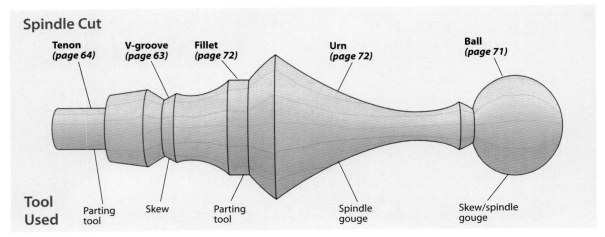

Tenon
(page 64)

V-groove
(page 63)

Fillet
(page 72)

Urn
(page 72)

Ball
(page 71)

Tool Used

Parting tool

Skew

Parting tool

Spindle gouge

Skew/spindle gouge

Spindle Cut

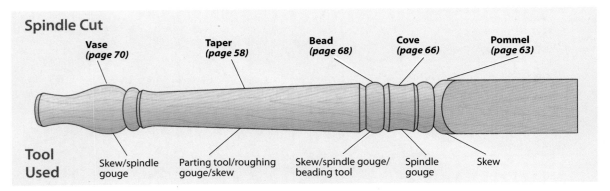

Vase
(page 70)

Taper
(page 58)

Bead
(page 68)

Cove
(page 66)

Pommel
(page 63)

Tool Used

Skew/spindle gouge

Parting tool/roughing gouge/skew

Skew/spindle gouge/ beading tool

Spindle gouge

Skew

Spindle Cut

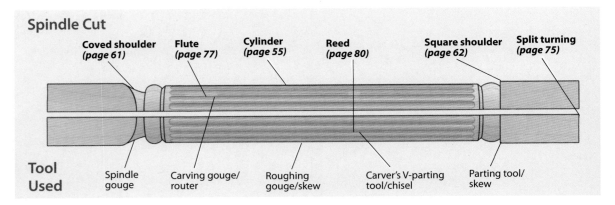

Coved shoulder
(page 61)

Flute
(page 77)

Cylinder
(page 55)

Reed
(page 80)

Square shoulder
(page 62)

Split turning
(page 75)

Tool Used

Spindle gouge

Carving gouge/ router

Roughing gouge/skew

Carver's V-parting tool/chisel

Parting tool/ skew

Setting Up

All spindle work starts with a square blank. The more perfect the square, the better. By starting with blanks that are straight, free of defects, squared on the jointer, and properly centered on the lathe, you can avoid catching a tool on the workpiece or splitting the wood.

Two keys to smooth spindle work are using proper tool control *(page 53)* and cutting in the direction of the wood grain *(page 54)*. Stance and body movement are just as important as how you hold a tool. A good working stance is to stand with your feet apart and comfortably balanced. Your body should be able to move smoothly with the tool. Never stand so far away from the lathe that you are forced to lean forward. With thicker workpieces, your hip or elbow can provide support for the tool.

While spindle turning is a relatively safe operation, remember not to become too casual in your approach. Improperly used, the lathe can cause injuries like any other woodworking machine.

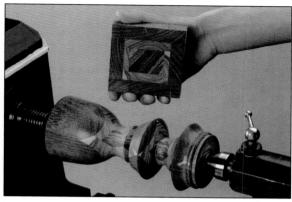

Laminated or "sandwich" blanks can yield interesting geometric patterns when they are turned between centers. The blank for the vase shown in the photo above was made by gluing layers of tulipwood and purpleheart around a square zebrawood core. A range of different patterns can be produced by alternating the manner in which the layers are glued up.

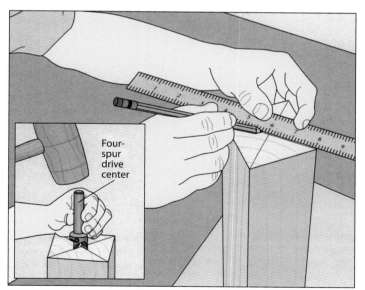

Four-spur drive center

Mounting a Blank between Centers

Marking the center of the blank

To mount a blank on the lathe for spindle turning, you need to find the center of each end. First make sure that the blank is square, then hold it on end and mark two lines across one end from corner to corner *(left)*. Repeat at the other end. The lines will intersect at the centers. Next, use a four-spur drive center and a mallet to make indentations at both points. Align the centerpoint of the drive center over the center on the end of the blank and strike it sharply with the mallet *(inset)*; make sure the spurs bite into the wood. Repeat at the other end. Insert the drive center in the headstock of the lathe. Do not strike the drive center while it is mounted in the headstock; this could damage the lathe's bearings.

Mounting the blank on the lathe

To mount the blank between centers, start by butting one end against the tailstock's live center. Supporting the other end of the blank with one hand, slide the tailstock towards the headstock until the spurs of the drive center engage with the indentations you made earlier. Secure the tailstock in place with the locking lever, then advance the tailstock spindle and live center by turning the handwheel until the blank is held firmly between the centers *(right)*. Secure the tailstock spindle in place with the spindle lock.

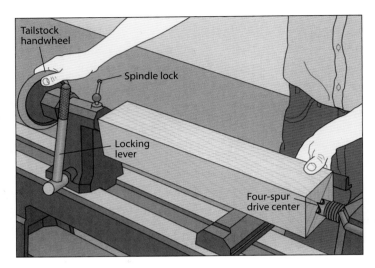

Tailstock handwheel

Spindle lock

Locking lever

Four-spur drive center

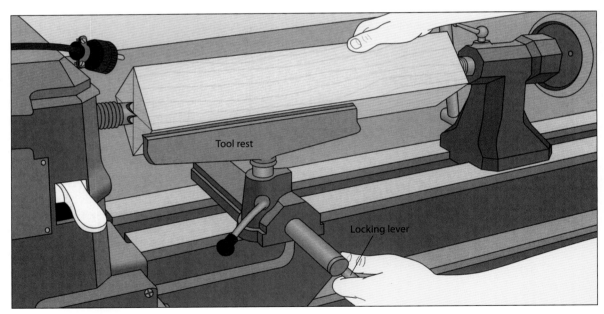

Tool rest

Locking lever

Adjusting the tool rest

Align the tool rest parallel to the blank, positioning it close to the workpiece without making contact when the blank spins. With the lathe switched off, rotate the blank by hand to ensure it does not hit the tool rest *(above)*. The gap between the tool rest and the blank should be the same at both ends; adjust the rest, if necessary. Although experienced turners adjust the height of the tool rest according to personal preference, a good place to start is with the tool rest at or slightly below the center of the blank. This way, your tools will cut above the center of the blank. Tighten the tool rest in position with the locking lever.

Basic Tool Control

Rubbing the bevel

The first rule of tool control in turning is to make sure the blade's bevel rubs against the stock as the cutting edge slices into the wood. This principle is the key to producing smooth, clean cuts with tools such as the spindle gouge and the skew chisel. To master this basic technique, unplug the lathe and mount a cylindrical blank between centers. Brace a tool—in this case a roughing gouge—on the tool rest so that its bevel rests on the stock. Gripping the tool with one hand, tilt the handle down. As shown at right, use your free hand to rotate the blank in a clockwise direction; the bevel should rub smoothly against the work.

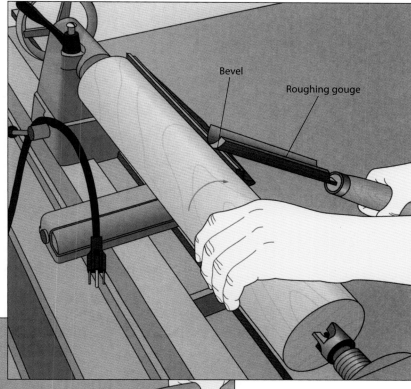

Bevel

Roughing gouge

Starting the cut

Once the bevel is rubbing, slowly raise the tool handle; the cutting edge should begin to slice the wood *(left)*. You can control the depth of cut by the height of the handle; the higher you raise it, the more wood you will remove. But do not go so far that the bevel stops rubbing against the wood, or the tool will catch on the spinning blank.

Making the cut

Slowly angle the tool in the direction of cut and slide it along the workpiece *(right)*, aligning your upper body behind the tool throughout the cut. As you move, rotate the tool slightly in the direction of cut to avoid catching the blade. Now, plug in the lathe, turn it on, and repeat with the blank spinning; the tool is cutting properly when you produce fine shavings and leave a smooth surface that requires little sanding.

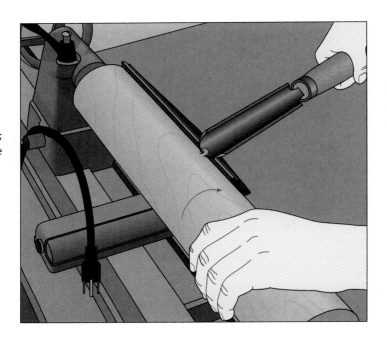

Cutting with the Wood Grain

Cutting "downhill"

Wood is composed of bundles of fibers aligned in one direction, called the grain direction. Just as pushing a hand plane against the grain will cause tearout, working against the grain with a turning tool will produce rough cuts and can lead to kickback. As shown by the arrows in the illustration at left, the smoothest spindle turning cuts are made in a downhill direction—from a high point to a low point on the workpiece. Such cuts are either with, across, or at an angle to the grain. Never cut uphill, or the tool will dig into the wood. This will cause splintering and shearing of wood fibers, and will leave a rough surface on the blank.

Basic Spindle Cuts

The basic spindle cuts shown in this section of the chapter will help sharpen your turning abilities for more challenging projects that you tackle later on. These cuts include roughing, planing, peeling, V-cuts, shoulder cuts, and parting off.

Four tools are used for most basic spindle cuts: the roughing gouge, the spindle gouge, the skew chisel, and the parting tool. They are typically held in one of two grips: overhand or underhand. The overhand grip is commonly used to guide a tool along the tool rest, such as when roughing down a blank *(below)*. The underhand grip is used for finer control, such as when making V-grooves *(page 60)*.

One bonus of spindle turning is that you can see the results of your cuts as you go. As you gain experience, you will also become familiar with the various sounds of the turning process. From your first roughing cuts to a final planing cut, there is a definite sequence of sounds produced as wood is being turned. By listening closely to

Because it is spinning at high speeds, a blank mounted between centers provides the turner with an immediate and continual visual check of a project's progress. In the photo above, a roughing gouge brings a small baseball bat to its final shape.

the succession of sounds emitted by the lathe, you will be able to use your ears—as well as your eyes—to assess the progress of your work.

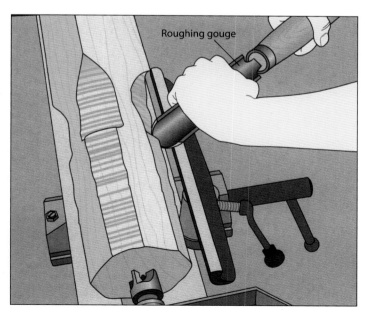

Roughing gouge

Turning a Cylinder

Roughing out the cylinder

Mount your blank between centers and set the appropriate speed for the size of the workpiece. Holding a roughing gouge with an overhand grip, brace the blade on the tool rest. Cut very lightly into the blank, making sure the bevel is rubbing against the stock and moving the gouge smoothly along the tool rest. (If your blank is longer than the tool rest, rough out the cylinder in two or more steps.) The gouge will begin rounding the corners of the workpiece *(left)*. Continue making successively deeper passes along the blank, raising the handle of the tool slightly with each pass, until the edges are completely rounded and you have a cylinder. Adjust the position of the tool rest as you progress to keep it close to the blank.

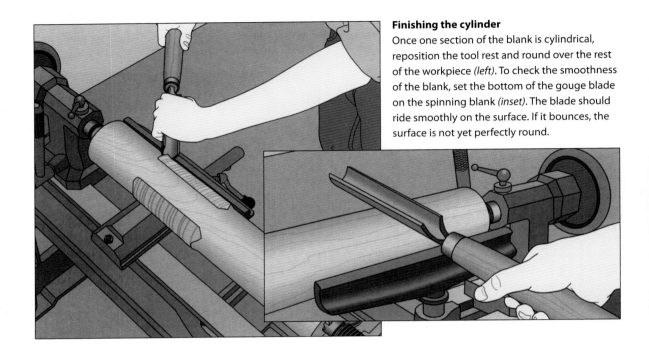

Finishing the cylinder

Once one section of the blank is cylindrical, reposition the tool rest and round over the rest of the workpiece *(left)*. To check the smoothness of the blank, set the bottom of the gouge blade on the spinning blank *(inset)*. The blade should ride smoothly on the surface. If it bounces, the surface is not yet perfectly round.

Planing the cylinder

Use a skew chisel to plane the cylinder to a smooth finish. Holding the tool with an overhand grip, set the blade on the rest so that its long point is above the blank and its bevel is inclined in the direction of the cut; this is typically about 65° to the axis of the wood. Switch on the lathe and raise the handle slightly, bringing the cutting edge of the chisel into contact with the wood. Move the blade along the tool rest *(right)*, letting its bevel rub; do not let its heel or long point dig into the wood. The center of the cutting edge should produce a series of thin shavings.

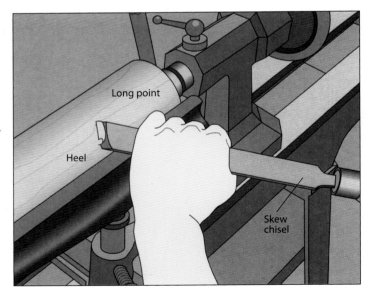

Long point

Heel

Skew chisel

Cutting the cylinder to length

Once you have planed the cylinder smooth, use a parting tool to cut it to length. Mark a cutting line on the spinning cylinder with a pencil. Then, holding a parting tool edge-up on the tool rest as shown at right, raise the handle slightly so the blade cuts into the blank. Clean up the end grain with a skew chisel *(page 62)*. If you have further shaping to do on the blank, cut about two-thirds of the way through the cylinder so that it remains on the lathe. If all you wish to make is a cylinder, continue the cut to near the center of the blank, then turn off the lathe and cut away the cylinder with a handsaw.

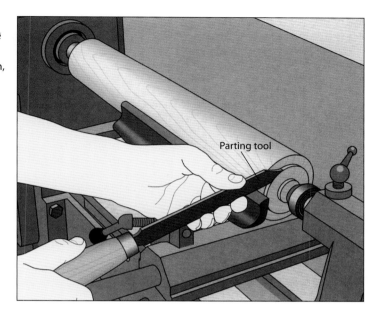

Parting tool

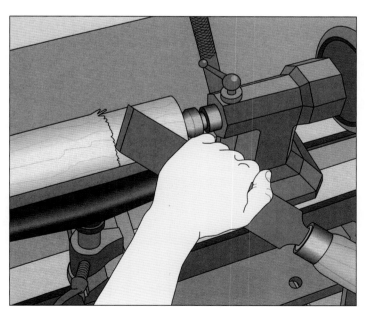

Peeling Cuts

Making a peeling cut

Peeling is an alternate way of quickly smoothing a cylinder; use a large skew chisel instead of a roughing gouge. A peeling cut is similar to a planing cut *(page 56)*, except that you intentionally dig the heel of the chisel into the blank with the bevel rubbing on the stock *(left)*. The heel will lift a circle of shavings as you guide the chisel along the tool rest. Because it removes a lot of stock and requires more control than a planing cut, peeling is more difficult to master, and should be done carefully.

Gauging Cutting Depth

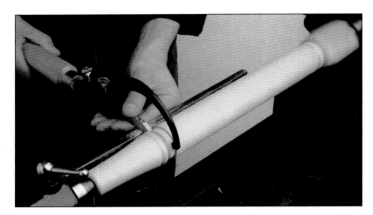

Attached to a parting tool, a sizing tool makes it easy to gauge the depth of cuts precisely. Set the gap between the parting tool's cutting edge and the knob on the sizing tool to the finished diameter. When cutting, the knob is always in contact with the blank; sizing cut is at desired depth when the knob slips behind the blank.

Making Tapers

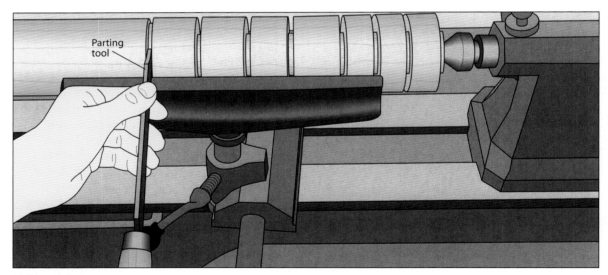

Parting tool

Making sizing cuts

If you are not copying a particular piece, make a hardboard template of the taper. (The template, illustrated on page 59, should indicate the finished diameter of the blank at several different points along its length.) Turn your blank into a cylinder *(page 55)*, then make a series of sizing cuts with a parting tool from one end of the blank to the other. Holding the parting tool with an underhand grip edge-up on the tool rest, raise the handle slightly so that the blade cuts into the cylinder. Continue to raise the handle until the cut reaches the required depth *(above)*. Each cut should penetrate to the finished diameter of the workpiece at that point; check your progress with calipers. Twist the tool slightly from side to side as you make the cut in order to minimize friction and to prevent the blade from jamming.

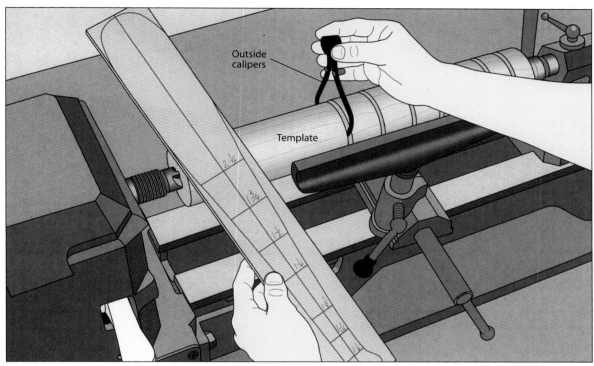

Outside
calipers

Template

Shop Tip

Using preset calipers

If you are spindle turning several identical pieces on the lathe, you can speed up the process by adjusting separate calipers for each feature of the blanks. For the leg shown here, one pair is adjusted for the thicker part of the leg, another is set for the bead below it, and a third is adjusted for the narrow section near the bottom of the leg. This will save you the trouble of continually readjusting a single pair of calipers. To avoid confusing the settings, attach a numbered strip of tape to each instrument.

Checking the depth of the sizing cuts

Adjust a pair of outside calipers to one of the dimensions of the taper as marked on your template. Then check the diameter of the blank at the corresponding sizing cut *(above)*. Deepen the cut if necessary until the measurements on the template and the diameter of the cut are equal. Repeat for the remaining sizing cuts.

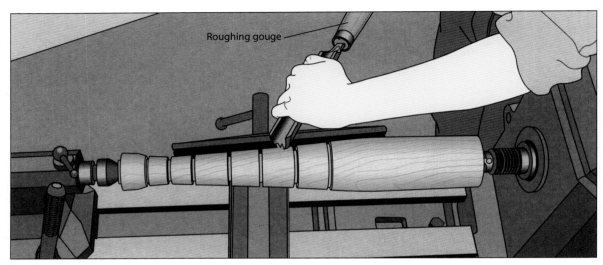

Roughing gouge

Roughing out the taper

Once you have finished all the sizing cuts, use a roughing gouge to clear out the waste between cuts. Follow the same procedure you would use to rough out a cylinder *(page 55)*, holding the tool with an overhand grip and always working in a downhill direction to avoid tearout *(above)*. Joining the sizing cuts will create a taper along the length of the workpiece. Then use a skew chisel to plane the taper smooth *(page 56)*. Work in a downhill direction.

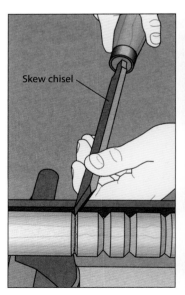

Skew chisel

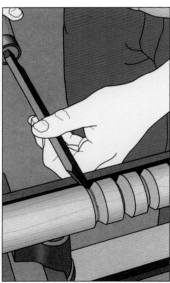

Grooving Cuts

Making decorative V-grooves

Turn a cylinder *(page 55)*, then mark the location of the grooves with a pencil. Make the cuts with a skew chisel. At each location mark, start with the long point of the chisel pointing forward and raise the handle, allowing the point of the blade to cut to the required depth. Then make a cut on each side of the initial cut, arcing the chisel to the side so a portion of the bevel rubs against the edge of the groove *(far left)*. To widen the groove, repeat the side cuts *(near left)*.

Coved Shoulder Cuts

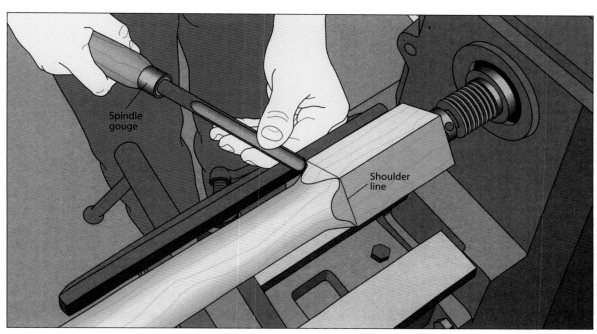

Spindle gouge

Shoulder line

Shop Tip

Preserving square shoulders

If you are spindle turning workpieces that require a sharp division between turned and square sections, such as the pommel at the top of a chair leg, wrap a length of duct or masking tape around the blank at the transition line before turning the cylinder. The tape provides a clear mark to where you should stop turning.

Turning the cove

Coved shoulders are a common feature of chair legs. To make the cut, start by scribing a shoulder line around the four sides of the blank to separate its round and square sections. Turn the round section of the blank to a cylinder *(page 55)*, tapering the leg if desired *(page 58)*. Next, use a spindle gouge to turn the coved shoulder. Holding the tool with an underhand grip at an angle to the blank, align its bevel with the direction of cut and its flute with the shoulder line. Raise the handle and pivot the tool on the tool rest, making a slicing cut "downhill," towards the tail stock end. Define the cove with a series of successively deeper cuts.

Square Shoulder Cuts

Turning the shoulder

Mark a shoulder line on the blank and turn the round section into a cylinder *(page 55)*, leaving the square section intact. Then use a skew chisel to clean up the transition between the square and round segments of the workpiece. Start by holding the tool edge up so that its long point and part of the bevel are aligned with the shoulder line. Slowly raise the handle, making a clean slicing cut down to the round portion of the workpiece *(right)*.

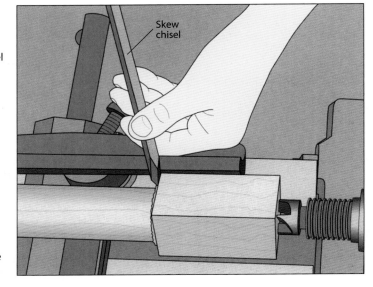

Skew chisel

Cleaning up the shoulder

Set the chisel's bevel flat on the round section and carefully touch the heel of the cutting edge against the shoulder to cut away any remaining waste *(below)*.

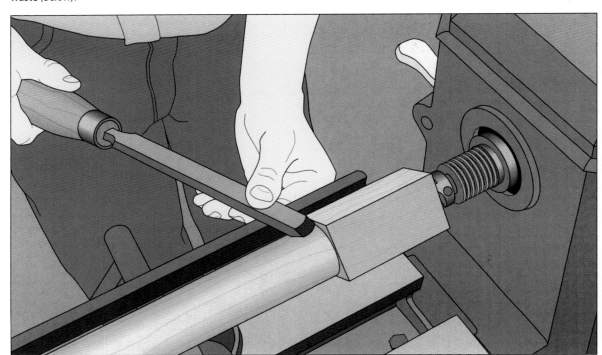

Turning Pommels

Cutting a V-groove

Mark a shoulder line around the four sides of a blank to separate the pommel from the cylindrical section of the leg. (For this procedure, the blank is turned into a cylinder after the pommel is cut.) Turn a V-groove in the workpiece with a skew chisel *(page 60)*, starting about ½ inch away from the shoulder line *(right)*. Deepen the groove until it runs completely around the workpiece.

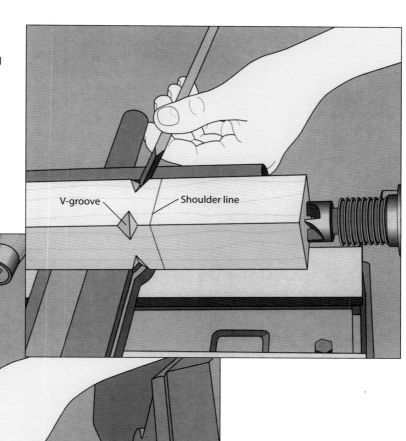

V-groove   Shoulder line

Shaping the pommel

Once you have finished the V-groove, turn the pommel as you would to widen the groove, cutting with the long point of the chisel pointed forward. Arc the chisel from side to side so the bevel rubs against the edges of the groove walls as you cut them *(left)*. Turn off the lathe after each cut to check the shape of the pommel; stop when you reach the shoulder line. Finally, turn the round portion of the workpiece into a cylinder *(page 55)*.

Parting Off

Parting off the workpiece

Once you have finished turning a spindle project, it may be necessary to separate it from the waste wood used to hold the workpiece between centers. For turnings with square ends, all you have to do is make a sizing cut *(page 58)* right through the workpiece with a parting tool. For turnings with rounded ends, like the urn finial shown at right, use a skew chisel or radiused skew chisel to preserve the curved shape. Holding the tool with an underhand grip, make a slicing cut with the long point of the blade as you would round a pommel *(page 63)*. Support the turning with your hand, keeping your fingers well clear of the tool rest and being careful not to grip the spinning workpiece. Make a series of deeper V-cuts until the finished turning breaks loose from the waste. Remove the workpiece from the lathe and saw off the waste at the other end.

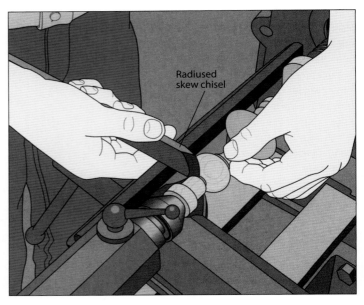

Radiused
skew chisel

Turning a tenon

If you intend to join your workpiece to another part of the finished work with a round mortise-and-tenon joint, turn a tenon at the end of the blank before parting it off. Holding a parting tool with an underhand grip, turn the tenon in the waste section of the blank *(left)*. Make a series of sizing cuts, checking the diameter of the tenon with calipers as you go.

Parting
tool

Thin Turnings

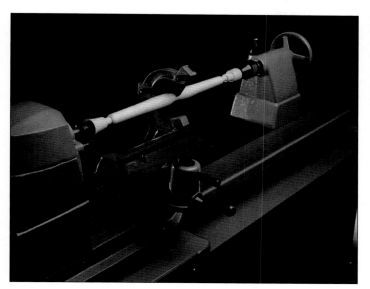

It is difficult to turn long, thin blanks between centers without gouging the surface because the turning will often flex and vibrate on the lathe, resulting in chatter. You can eliminate this problem by using a commercial steady rest, which supports thin spindle work between centers. The model shown in the photo at left slides along the lathe bed and adjusts for turnings up to 2¼ inches in diameter.

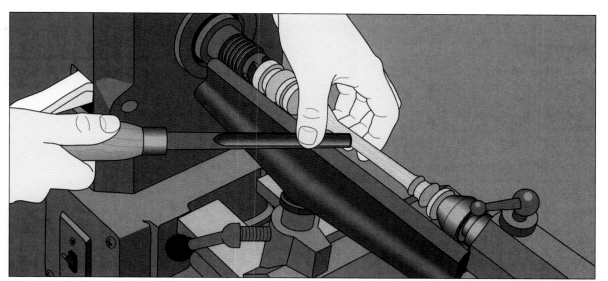

Supporting thin spindle work

When shaping thin spindle work, such as the honey dripper shown above, it is important to support the workpiece and reduce vibration. If you do not have a steady rest, you can use one of your hands. As you turn the blank, cradle it in the fingers of your left hand while bracing the tool against the rest with the thumb *(above)*. Keep your fingers clear of the tool blade and avoid applying excessive pressure on the turning.

Decorative Spindle Cuts

Unlike basic spindle turning, which is primarily concerned with roughing, sizing, and smoothing cylindrical or tapered furniture parts, decorative spindle work involves elaboration—cutting grooves, notches, curves, and other shapes. But despite its apparent complexity, nearly all decorative spindle turning is based on two fundamental cuts: coves and beads. Coves *(below)* are concave hollows turned in workpieces, while beads *(page 68)* have the opposite profile: a convex surface raised from the surrounding work. Although coves and beads can stand alone, they are often part of a series of elements in an overall turning design.

The spindle gouge and skew chisel are the two main tools you will use. With its fingernail-ground bevel, the spindle gouge is a good tool for smoothing the convex and concave profiles of beads and coves. The skew chisel is normally used to cut beads. Just as practicing basic spindle cuts can sharpen your turning technique, cutting

Decorative elements can sometimes be formed in spindle stock without the aid of turning tools. In the photo above, a length of light-gauge wire burns grooves into a child's rattle as the stock is spun at high speed.

coves and beads will prepare you for the challenge of such elaborate decorative cuts as vases and balls *(page 71)*. To size these elements, and repeat patterns successfully, you can use a template, a reverse-image of the desired shape.

Cutting Coves

Making the first cut

Outline the cove on the blank with a pencil. Then, hold a spindle gouge in an underhand grip with the flute pointing sideways and slice into the wood just inside one of the marked lines with the cutting edge of the tool only. Slowly angle the tool handle back towards the line until the bevel rubs on the workpiece, and make a scooping cut down to the middle of the cove. As you make the cut, turn the handle to rotate the bevel against the workpiece *(right)*. The gouge should be flat on its back when it reaches the center of the cove. Rather than continuing the cut and turning the remaining half of the cove in an uphill direction, make a second downhill cut opposite the first.

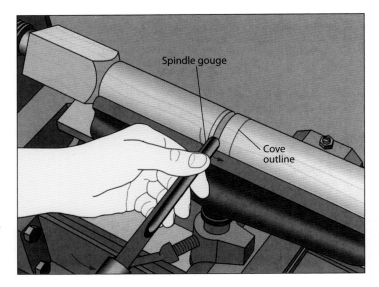

Spindle gouge

Cove outline

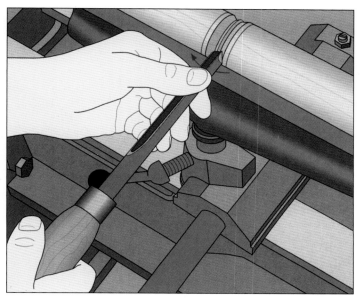

Making the second cut

With the gouge on its side and positioned inside the the other marked line for the cove, start the new cut as you did the first one. Then angle and rotate the spindle gouge in the opposite direction to bring the bevel in contact with the stock *(left)*.

Widening the cove

Repeat the first two steps, making a series of deeper cuts from right and left that meet at the bottom of the cove *(below)*. Continue cutting back to the marked lines until the cove is complete.

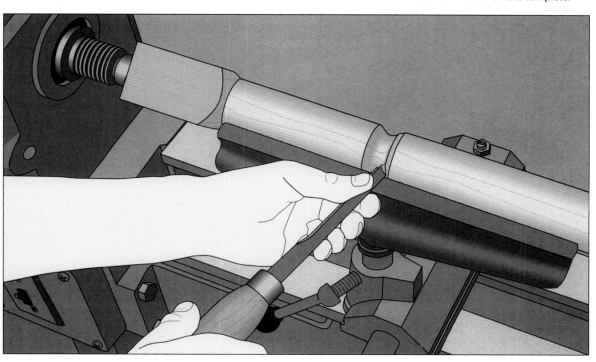

Turning Beads: Spindle Gouge

Turning the bead
Decorative beads can be turned with spindle
gouges, skew chisels *(page 69)*, or beading tools
(page 70). With the gouge, the technique for
turning beads is the reverse of cutting coves,
reflecting the difference in their profiles. Start by
outlining the bead on your blank with a pencil.
Beginning at the center—or highest point—of
the bead, hold the gouge flat and perpendicular
to the work so that its bevel is rubbing. Raise the
handle and make a downhill cut, rotating the
tool in the direction of cut and angling it away
from the cut *(right)*. The gouge should finish the
cut resting on its side. Repeat for the other side
of the bead, angling and rolling the tool in the
opposite direction.

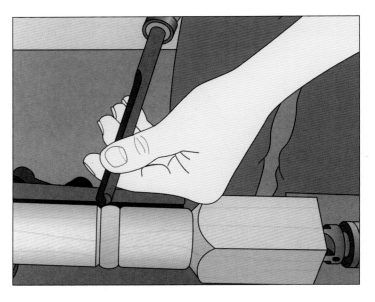

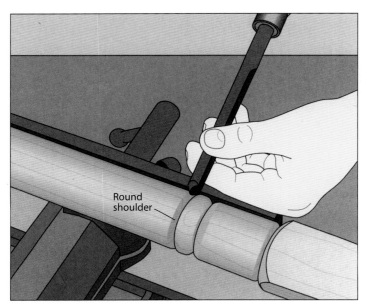

Round
shoulder

Turning round shoulders
Whether the bead will stand alone or be part
of a series of beads, blend it into the turning
by making round shoulders on each side of it.
Simply repeat to turn a half-bead beside the full
bead *(left)*.

Turning Beads: Skew Chisel

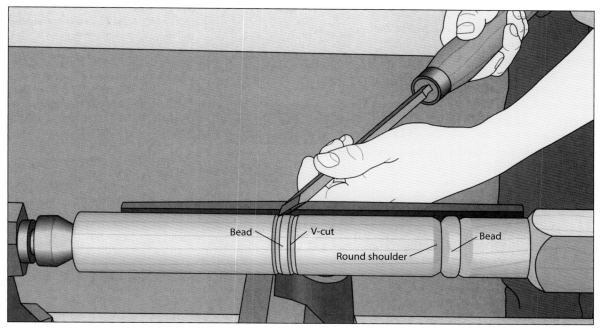

Bead
V-cut
Round shoulder
Bead

Defining the bead

A skew chisel enables you to turn beads with sharp detail. Outline the bead with a pencil, then make a V-cut *(page 60)* at each line. You can use either the long or short point of the chisel, but the long point, as shown here, usually makes the job easier. Then, working on one of the V-cuts, widen one side of the cut, slowly lifting the handle so the bevel rubs and the long point of the chisel makes a rounded, rolling cut. Repeat for the other side of the bead *(above)*.

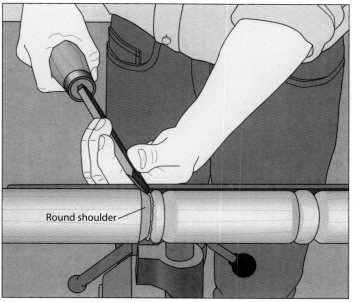

Round shoulder

Completing the bead

Repeat as necessary to smooth the bead's shape. Then turn a round shoulder on each side of the bead to blend it into the other elements of the turning *(left)*.

Turning Beads: Beading Tool

Making the cut

Because its blade is smaller, a beading tool provides even finer control for turning small beads than either a spindle gouge or a skew chisel. The process is similar to using a skew chisel. Starting at the center—or highest point—of the bead, hold the tool flat and perpendicular to the blank so that its bevel is rubbing. Raise the handle and make a downhill cut, rotating the tool in the direction of cut and angling it away. The beading tool should come to rest on its side. Repeat for the other side of the bead, angling and rolling the tool in the opposite direction.

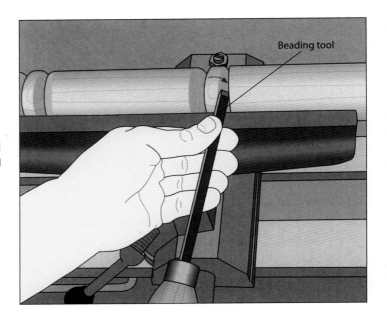

Beading tool

Resembling a teardrop-shaped bead, the vase is a design element often incorporated in balusters and chair legs. The bottom of the vase is cut like a bead with a skew chisel and shaped with rolling cuts. In the photo at left, the neck is being shaped with a spindle gouge using the cove-cutting technique.

Turning a Ball

Shaping the ball

A ball is a spherical bead that usually stands alone on a spindle turning like the chair leg shown at right. The decorative detail can be turned with a skew chisel, a spindle gouge, or a beading tool. Start by shaping the elements around the ball, then define the ball itself with a spindle gouge as you would a bead *(page 68)*, but making it wider and fuller. Starting at the center—or highest point—of the ball, hold the gouge flat and perpendicular to the work so that its bevel is rubbing. Lift the handle and make a downhill cut, rotating the tool in the direction of cut and angling it away. The gouge should come to rest on its side. Repeat for the other side of the ball *(right)*, angling and rolling the tool in the opposite direction.

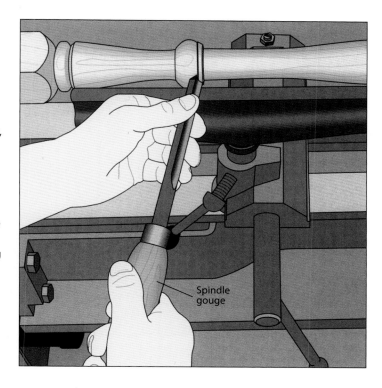

Spindle gouge

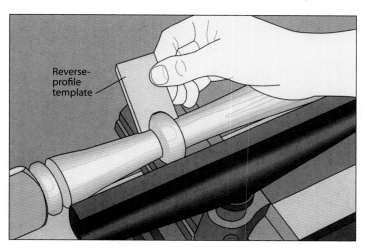

Reverse-profile template

Sizing with a template

To check the shape of the ball, cut a small reverse-profile template from hardboard with the desired curve of the ball *(left)*. If necessary, make a few more rolling cuts with the spindle gouge until the ball matches the profile of the template.

Spindle Turning

Back to **Basics**

Turning Fillets

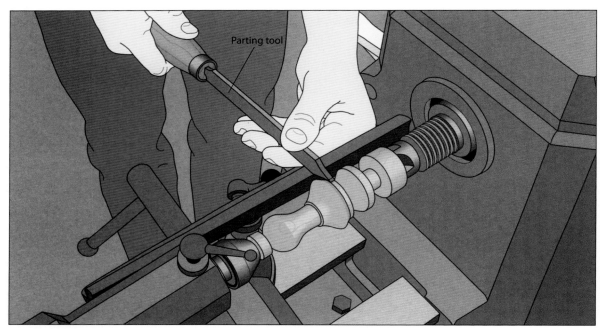

Cutting a fillet

A fillet is a flat segment that joins two decorative elements of a turning. In the illustration above, a fillet is being turned between a cove and an urn. To cut a fillet, hold a parting tool with an underhand grip and make a sizing cut *(page 58)*.

Finials

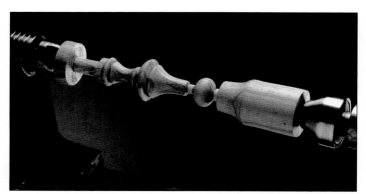

Incorporating many decorative spindle cuts into a unified whole, finials add the crowning touch to furniture pieces such as highboys, beds, and balusters. The tulipwood finial in the photo at left features a ball-and-urn motif with coves, beads, and fillets as transitional elements.

Handles for Turning Tools

Turning your own tool handles is more than just good spindle practice. Some turning tools are sold without handles, and many turners prefer to make their own to fit their hands.

To turn a tool handle, cut a blank from a dense, strong hardwood such as ash or hickory, making sure that the grain runs along the length of the blank. A blank that is 1½ to 2 inches square and 13 to 16 inches long will yield a standard handle. Mount the piece between centers and turn it down to a smooth cylinder.

Buy a brass ferrule for the handle, or make one from 1-inch-diameter copper tubing, cut about 1 inch long. File the edges smooth. Then use a parting tool to turn a tenon on one end of the blank to accommodate the ferrule.

Measure the inside diameter of the ferrule with dial calipers (right, top), and turn the outside diameter of the tenon to match. Give the tenon a slight taper so the ferrule will fit snugly. Remove the handle from the lathe, set it end down on a work surface, and tap the ferrule in place with a mallet (right, bottom).

Next, remount the handle on the lathe and shape it with a skew chisel and spindle gouge.

As you are turning the handle, switch off the lathe occasionally and check how the handle feels in your hand. If you wish, make decorative grooves in the tail end of the handle; some wood turners identify their tools according to the number of grooves in the handle.

Once you are satisfied with the handle's shape, you need to bore a hole in the tenon

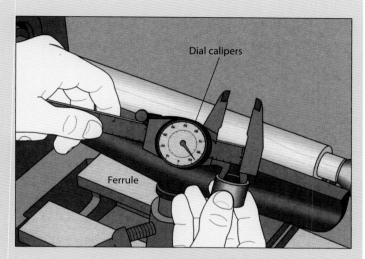

Dial calipers

Ferrule

end to accommodate the tang of the tool. The size of the hole depends on the type of tang. For round-section, untapered tangs, bore a hole equal to the tang diameter 2 to 3 inches deep. For square-section, tapered tangs, you need to drill a two-step hole: The top half should be the same diameter as the tang 1¼ inches from the tip; the bottom half should be the same width as the tang ¾ inch from its tip.

Bore the holes on the lathe. Mount the bit in a Jacobs chuck and attach the chuck to the lathe tailstock. Holding the handle steady, advance the tailstock and handle with the handwheel so the bit bores straight into the tenon end (page 49). Make sure the hole is centered in the blank.

To complete the handle, saw off the waste at the butt end and insert the blade into the handle. Secure the blade in place by rapping the butt of the handle with a mallet.

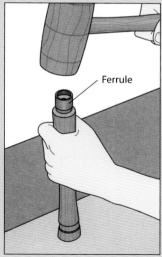

Ferrule

Duplicate Turnings

Using a story template

When making multiple copies of a single design, such as a series of table legs, a story template will help you outline the pattern on each blank. To make the template, draw your design full-scale on a piece of ⅛-inch hardboard. Mark a centerline down the length of the template, then outline each element in the turning—beads, coves, fillets, balls, urns, vases—by marking lines perpendicular to the centerline. Also mark the desired thickness of each element on the template. To use the template, hold it on the tool rest and butt one edge against the blank. Turn on the lathe and transfer the marked lines from the template to the spinning blank with a pencil (*right*). The resulting lines will provide a guide to the location of each element on the workpiece. As the turning progresses, use calipers to check the blank against the measurements on the template.

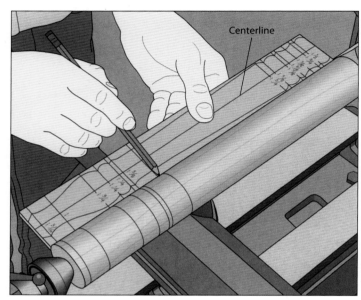

Centerline

Shop Tip

A layout tool for multiple turnings

For multiple copies of spindle work, the shop-made layout jig shown here enables you to scribe layout lines on every blank quickly and accurately. Trace your design onto a piece of scrap and drive a finishing nail into the edge of the jig at each transition in the design. Snip off the nail heads and file the ends to sharp points. Once you have shaped your blank into a cylinder, simply press the jig against it; the nails will score all the layout lines on the blank at once.

Split and Carved Turnings

Decorative spindle turning does not end with beads, coves, and balls. With a little imagination, exotic touches can be added to an ordinary spindle turning. One innovative technique involves cleaving a turning down the middle, producing symmetrical halves. Ideal for pieces such as bookends, wall-mounted lamps, or quarter columns, split spindle turning is an easy technique to master. The blank is sawn in half or quarters, glued up with newspaper in the joint, and mounted in the lathe. After the workpiece is turned, the pieces can be easily separated.

Reeds and flutes made along the length of a spindle turning are two other popular decorative elements. In fact, reeds and flutes date to ancient Greek and Roman times, and later became cornerstones of the Sheraton style of furniture in the mid-18th Century.

Carved in balusters, chair legs, and bedposts, reeds and flutes guide the eye along the piece and accentuate its vertical line. Reeds *(page 80)* are convex and are typically carved into a taper or vase to accentuate its curve. Flutes *(page 77)* are concave and are ordinarily cut into cylinders. They are frequently a feature of quarter columns.

Both reeds and flutes can be carved on a blank while it is still mounted in the lathe, although not while the lathe is actually running. The machine's indexing head enables

Quarter columns add a visual framework to fine furniture such as the Queen Anne chest of drawers shown above. The columns are made from a single blank sawn in four, then glued up, turned on the lathe, and pried apart.

you to space the reeds or flutes equally while holding the workpiece stationary as you carve. You also can rout flutes with an electric router and the jig shown on page 78.

Making a Split Turning

Gluing up the blank

To prepare a blank for a split turning, cut the piece oversize. If you will be splitting the turning in two, as for the pair of bell-shaped bookends shown on page 76, saw the blank in half. For quarter columns rip the blank into four equal pieces *(inset)*. Joint the inside surfaces of each blank, then glue and clamp them back together with newspaper in between *(left)*. This will allow you to pull the pieces apart easily. Once the glue is dry, remove the clamps, mount the blank on the lathe, and turn it.

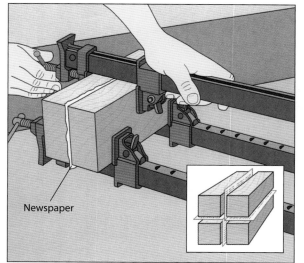

Newspaper

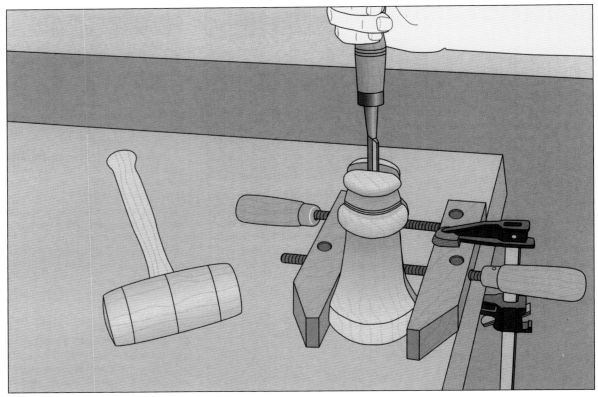

Separating the turning

After the turning has been finished, remove it from the lathe. Then use a wood chisel to pry the glued-up halves apart. Secure the turning to a work surface as shown above, then work the chisel into the seam on the end of the stock. Tap the chisel gently with a mallet and twist the blade from side to side until the pieces separate. Clean the glue and newspaper from the inside surfaces with a scraper.

Shop Tip

Using compression rings

Split turnings can break apart before you are finished turning them. One way to solve the problem is to reinforce the blanks with shop-made compression rings. Cut two ¼-inch-long rings from 1½-inch-diameter copper tubing and sharpen one rim of each with a file. Before mounting the blank, drive a ring into each end with a hammer, as shown here.

Making Flutes

Outlining the flutes

Use the lathe's indexing head and a shop-made layout jig to mark the flutes on your blank. For the jig, attach the upright to the base piece at a 90° angle. Bore a hole through the upright to hold a pencil tip level with the middle of the blank when the base is set on the lathe bed. Insert the indexing pin into the indexing head to secure the headstock and blank. Slide the layout jig along the lathe bed, marking the flute on the leg. To space the flutes equally, you must rotate the indexing head by the same amount each time you mark out a flute. Divide the number of holes in the head—in this case, 60—by the number of flutes you want. If you wanted six flutes, for example, you would rotate the head by 10 holes. Remove the pin from the head, rotate the head the required number of holes, and mark the second flute *(right)*. Repeat until all the flutes are marked. To outline the flutes for carving, mark two equally spaced lines on each side of the flute centerline mark, forming a narrow rectangle.

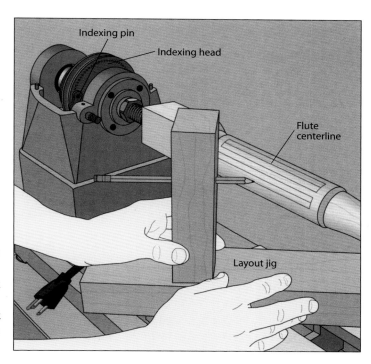

Indexing pin

Indexing head

Flute centerline

Layout jig

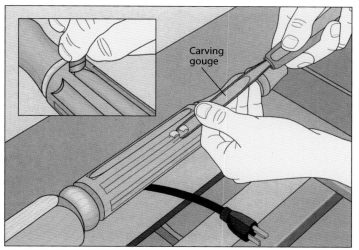

Carving gouge

Carving the flutes

With the leg still mounted in the lathe, use a carving gouge to fashion the flutes. For each flute, secure the leg with the indexing pin and cut a shallow channel along the centerline with the gouge. Make a series of deeper cuts with the gouge, maintaining an even depth along the flute *(left)*. To finish, make a plunge cut with the carving gouge at each end of the flute with the bevel facing the middle of the flute *(inset)*. Then clean up the corners of the cuts with the gouge.

A Column-Fluting Jig

The jig shown at right will enable you to use a router for cutting flutes on your lathe turnings. Cut the pieces of the jig from ¾-inch plywood, except for the top, which is made from ¼-inch clear acrylic. The jig should be long and wide enough to support your router's base plate, and high enough to hold the tool just above the blank when the jig is set on the lathe bed.

Assemble the top, bottom, and sides, then add the braces for rigidity. Install a double-bearing piloted fluting bit in your router, bore a bit clearance hole through the jig top, and screw the tool's base plate to the jig.

To space the flutes equally, you can use the indexing head method described on page 77 or mark the flutes on a faceplate. If you want 12 flutes, for example, divide 360 (the number of degrees in a circle) by 12, yielding a space of 30°. Use a protractor and a pencil to mark flute lines on the faceplate

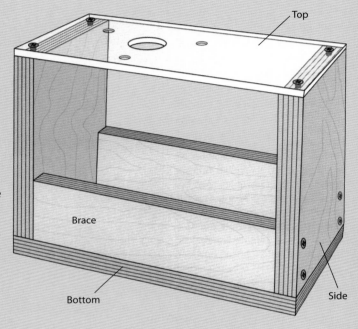

Top

Brace

Bottom

Side

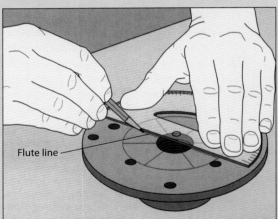

Flute line

30° apart *(left)*. Attach the faceplate to the headstock of the lathe.

To set up the jig, place it on the lathe bed and mount the blank between centers; make sure that the lathe and router are unplugged. Also ensure that the glue lines separating the parts of the blank are aligned with the flute marks on the faceplate. Set the router's depth of cut so that the bit is centered along the horizontal axis of the blank. Rotate the faceplate by hand until one of the flute lines is at the 12 o'clock position. Tighten a handscrew around the lathe drive shaft to prevent it from rotating.

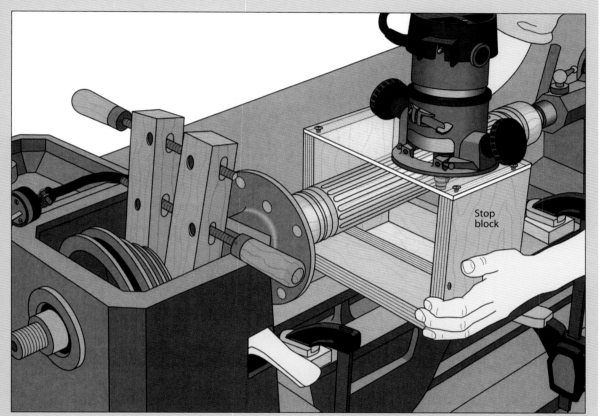

Stop block

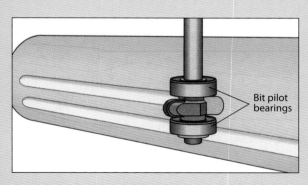

Bit pilot bearings

To be certain that all the flutes will be the same length, clamp stop blocks to the lathe bed. Butt the jig against one stop block, turn on the router, and push on the side of the jig to feed the bit into the blank. Once the pilots are bearing against the stock *(left)*, slide the jig along the lathe bed until it contacts the other stop block. Keep the bit pilots pressed against the stock as it routs the flute.

Turn off the router, remove the hand-screw, and rotate the faceplate by hand to align the next flute line with the bit, then reinstall the handscrew. Repeat to cut the remaining flutes *(above)*.

Making Reeds

Marking out the reeds

Outline reeds on a turning blank using your lathe's indexing head as you would mark flutes. You can use a layout jig *(page 77)* or the tool rest. With the lathe unplugged and the indexing pin in the head, position the rest parallel to the blank and raise it so the top of the rest is level with the middle of the blank. Draw a pencil along the tool rest to lay out the first reed. To mark each remaining reed *(right)*, disengage the pin from the indexing head, rotate the head, and reinsert the pin in the appropriate hole.

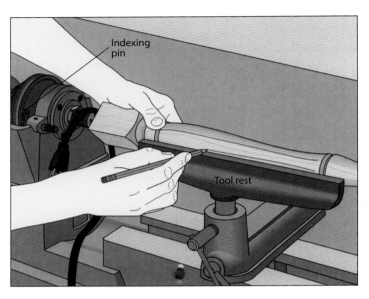

Indexing pin

Tool rest

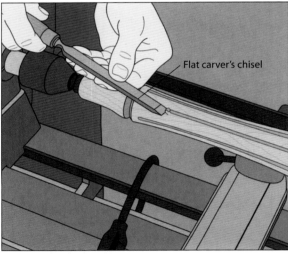

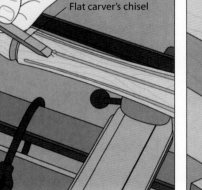

Flat carver's chisel

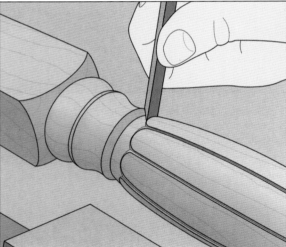

Carving the reeds

Use a well-sharpened carver's parting tool to outline the reeds. Secure the leg on the lathe with the indexing pin so that one of your layout lines is facing upwards, then cut a shallow groove along the line with the parting tool. Repeat for the other marked lines, then round the reeds between them by making cuts on each side of the grooves, rolling a flat carver's chisel slightly from side to side *(above, left)*. Follow the leg's contours, making the reeds wider at the top than at the bottom. End the tops of the reeds as you did the flutes, using a carving gouge of the proper size *(above, right)*; the bottoms of reeds are often left open.

Finishing

There is a widespread belief among wood turners that if a turning needs to be sanded, then the tools used to produce it were either dull or used improperly. There is more than a little truth behind this opinion; a smooth and clean turning needs no sanding. A surface cut cleanly by tools is superior to a sanded surface; sanding inevitably scratches a spindle turning because it is performed against the grain. To make matters worse, a finish will only magnify the blemishes.

Until you develop into a proficient enough turner to skip sandpaper altogether, use it sparingly, only to smooth the wood, never to actually shape it. Start with 100 grit and work up to 280 grit. Wherever possible, sand the bottom of the turning as it spins on the lathe. Should the paper catch, it will be thrown clear of the lathe instead of pulling your hand over the turning.

A spindle turning is best finished right on the lathe. A good finish seals the wood from dust and moisture while bringing out the natural beauty of the wood. Because they tend to obscure rather than enhance grain, stains are rarely used. Turnings are often finished with a combination oil-and-wax finish, although higher-gloss finishes, such as lacquer, can be applied; see the chart below for a selection of appropriate products. As with sanding on the lathe, run the machine at a slow speed to avoid splashing,

The simplest and most natural finish for a spindle turning is often the one closest at hand. In the photo above, a cherry finial is being rubbed with a palm-full of wood shavings. Natural oils from the shavings will impart a warm, burnished glow to the wood.

always keep the tool rest clear of the work and finish the turning from underneath. Avoid using large cloths, as they can get snagged and pull your fingers into the spinning work.

A Selection of Finishes for Turning

Type of Finish	Finishing Products	Characteristics and Uses	Methods of Application
Penetrating oils	Tung oil, Danish oil	Natural finish that penetrates the wood and hardens to a thin, moisture-resistant film as it dries. Used for general spindle turnings, penetrating oils build up a transparent matte to semigloss finish with repeated applications.	Applied with cotton cloth.
Non-toxic penetrating oils	Pure walnut oil, salad oil, mineral oil	These are natural oils. Pure walnut oil and salad oil are used on kitchen implements and salad bowls, mineral oil is used on turned toys such as children's rattles.	Applied with cotton cloth.
High-gloss finishes	Lacquer, shellac	Solvent-release finishes that dry quickly to a clear, hard finish; a glossy finish can be built up with repeated applications. Used on vases, bowls, platters and specialty turnings where a high gloss is desired.	Lacquer is brushed or sprayed on turning while lathe is off, then buffed and burnished with cotton cloth and fine abrasives while work is spinning; shellac is applied with cotton cloth and fine abrasives.
Waxes	Carnauba, beeswax, paste wax	Used on general spindle turnings to seal and protect oiled workpieces while imparting a high polish. Carnauba is a hard, brittle vegetable wax; commercial paste wax is a blend of carnauba and softer beeswax.	Applied with cotton cloth; carnauba can be applied by stick.

Smoothing a Spindle Turning

Sanding a flat section

Remove the tool rest. To sand the flat areas of a spindle turning, fold a piece of sandpaper in thirds to prevent the paper from slipping. Switch on the lathe and, holding the paper in both hands, lift the paper to the turning from underneath. Work with the grain along the length of the work as much as possible *(right)*. Stop sanding periodically to prevent burning. Once the scratches from the previous grit have been smoothed away, move to a finer paper.

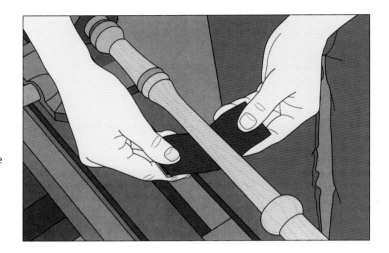

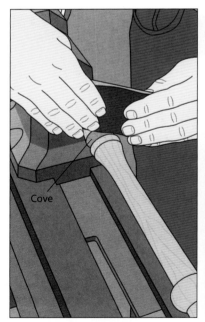

Cove

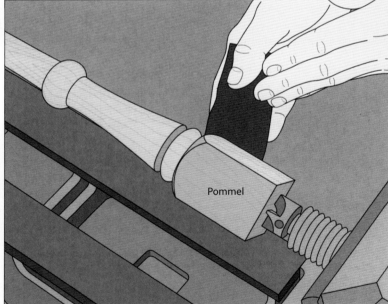

Pommel

Sanding coves, beads and pommels

Coves are sanded by bending the sandpaper into a U shape so the paper contacts the concave surface. Holding the paper in both hands, smooth the cove from directly above *(above, left)*. Narrow coves can be sanded by wrapping the paper around a dowel of the appropriate diameter. Sand beads or pommels holding the paper vertically and rolling from side to side to contact the wood *(above, right)*. Be careful that your fingers are not struck by the square pommel corners.

Finishing a Spindle Turning

Oiling the turning

Set the lathe to a slow speed to prevent the oil from splashing. Apply some oil to a soft cotton cloth and rub it into the spinning wood from underneath *(right)*; make sure the cloth is not wrapped around your fingers. Let the turning dry, and repeat as many times as needed until the oil penetrates the wood. If desired, you can sand the turning with 320-grit sandpaper and rub out the finish with fine abrasives such as pumice or rottenstone and a rag. Finally, rub the turning with wood shavings *(photo, page 81)* to give it a final burnishing.

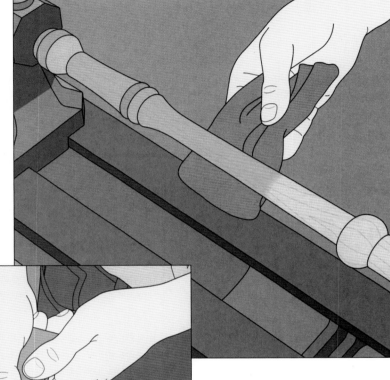

Wax
stick

Waxing the turning

To give the turning a higher polish, increase the lathe speed and apply a wax finish. If you are using a soft wax, apply it with a soft cloth as you would oil. If you are using a turner's wax stick, hold the stick gently against the spinning workpiece *(left)*, applying a thin layer to the surface. Move the wax stick quickly along the turning to prevent too much buildup. With either wax, buff the turning with a clean cotton cloth; keep rubbing until the wax is melted and the desired gloss is achieved.

Faceplate Turning

There is something uniquely rewarding about faceplate turning—transforming a piece of rough lumber into a smooth, symmetrical bowl. From start to finish, the entire process takes place on a lathe. There is no assembly, joinery, or fabrication of other parts. The product is complete in this single process.

Faceplate turning also offers the wood turner a great deal of design freedom. True, there are certain practical considerations. What will the bowl hold? How strong does it need to be? But there is also much room for experimentation and improvisation in distinguishing factors ranging from the shape of the bowl and its base to the thickness of its walls.

The options increase with a turner's skill. For beginners, it is best first to master some traditional shapes and profiles. This chapter will show how to produce two relatively easy bowl designs. Completing these projects will help you develop the skills that you will need to give free reign to your creativity.

Most bowl-turning projects follow the same basic sequence. Begin by mounting what will be the top of the bowl to the lathe, then shape the outside, sand and finish the surface, and prepare the base for mounting. Then reverse the bowl and true and shape the rim. Finally, turn the inside of the bowl, sand and finish it, and reverse the bowl one last time to complete the base and remove evidence of your mounting method.

Before you begin turning, you will need to find a suitable way to mount your blank on the lathe. Traditionally, this is done by screwing or taping the stock to a faceplate or gluing it to a block attached to the faceplate. More recently, turners have used a variety of chucks to clamp their work. Chucks can hold small and oddly shaped pieces, and are excellent for gripping the rim of a bowl to turn the base. Chucks also can save you time if you are turning a series of similar pieces. No matter what you use to hold a blank, you are sure to find faceplate turning a rewarding and challenging experience.

Once a bowl is turned and sanded smooth, a finish can be applied. Because the bowl shown here is intended to hold food, it is given a light coating of mineral oil with a lint-free cotton pad.

A gouge shapes the base of a bowl. The recess at the center of the base will be used to rechuck the bowl to the lathe so the inside can be hollowed out.

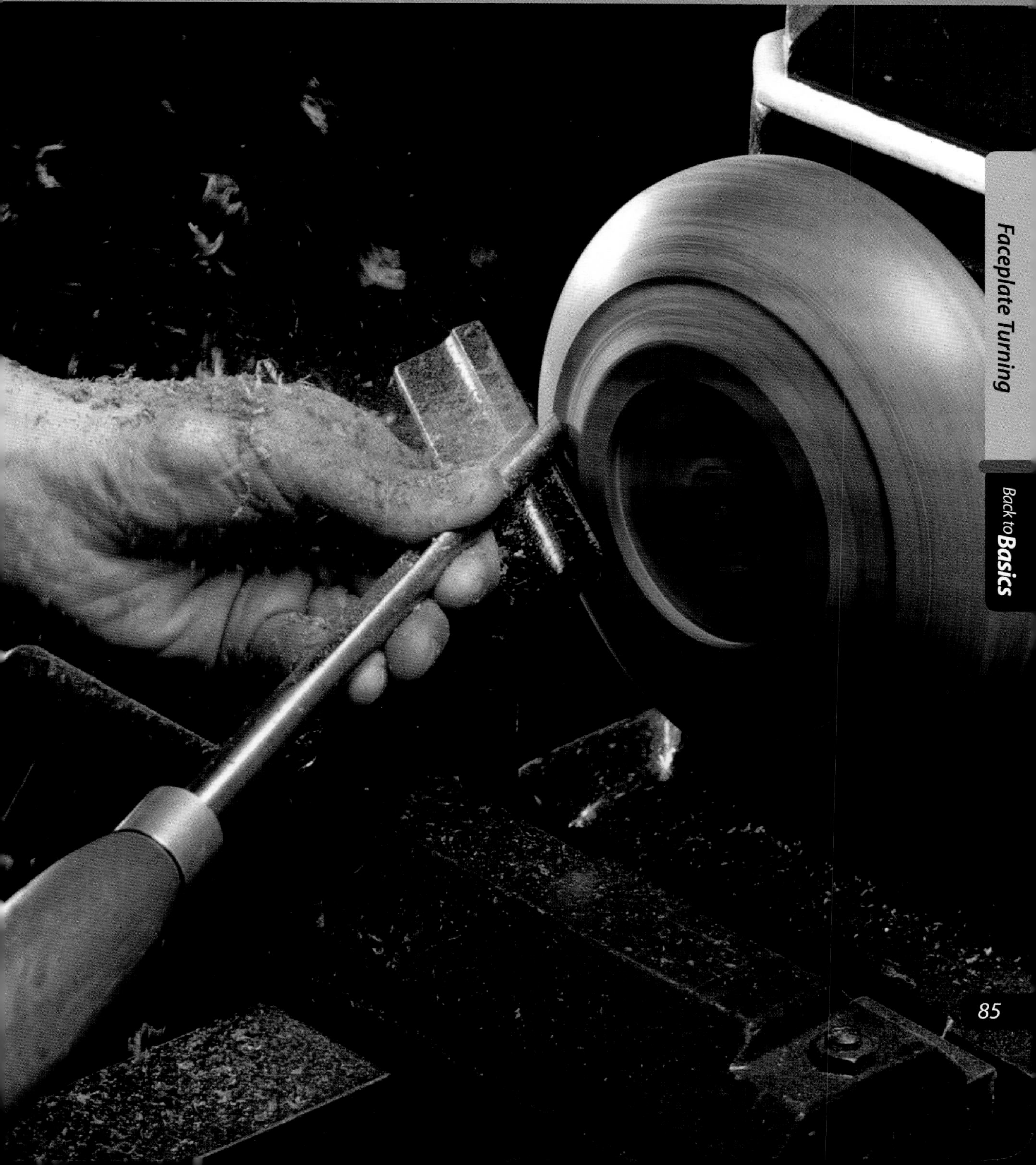

Mounting Methods

The methods of mounting a blank for faceplate turning far outnumber the techniques used to produce the pieces themselves. The traditional work-holding device, the faceplate *(below)*, is still popular for securing the top of a bowl to turn the bottom; screws are driven into wood that will be hollowed out later to form the mouth of the vessel. Rather than driving screws into your blank, you can use a faceplate for mounting with a glue block *(page 87)*, a paper joint *(page 87)*, or double-sided tape *(page 88)*. Once the turning is finished, the workpiece is pried, sawn, or parted off the auxiliary block—or, in the case of double-sided tape, the faceplate. In general, yellow glue should be used with glue blocks except when you are turning green wood, for which gap-filling cyanoacrylate adhesive is the best choice.

The alternative to a faceplate is a chuck, and the number of commercial models available to wood turners has increased in recent years. Most standard chucking methods are shown in the following pages. The scroll chuck *(page 90)*, which uses three or four contracting or expanding jaws to clamp stock, is a prime example. It is quick and easy to use and the jaws leave no visible marks on the workpiece. In addition, some models can be fitted with rubber posts for holding the rim of a nearly finished bowl so the bottom can be turned *(page 112)*. However, the spinning jaws represent a two-fold danger. First, if you get too close, they can inflict a serious wound. Second, and most important, if you over-expand the jaws, they can come loose and fly away from the tool, causing injury.

If you use a chuck, read the owner's manual carefully and follow all the safety precautions, particularly those regarding the size of the workpiece and the chuck capacity. Commercial chucks can also be expensive. The shop-made example shown on page 92 is handy and costs almost nothing to build. Other traditional wooden chuck designs can be made just as easily and tailored for your work.

Faceplates

Mounting the blank
A faceplate provides a reliable and safe method of mounting stock to the headstock, but you must be careful not to drive screws into any wood that will remain in the finished bowl. Rough-cut your blank to a circle on the band saw, then set it on a work surface. Center the faceplate on top of the bowl blank and fasten it in place *(right)*. Then, mount the faceplate to the headstock spindle of the lathe.

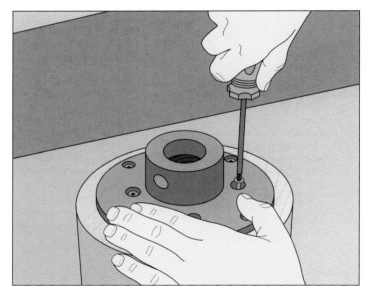

Glue Blocks

Clamping a glue block to the blank

The glue block mounting method relies on adhesives that provide a solid hold without penetrating too deeply into the wood. Usually, yellow glue will do the job. Make sure the bottom of the bowl blank is even enough to form a clean joint with the glue block; smooth the surface with a hand plane, if necessary. To fashion the glue block, cut a wood block into a circle slightly larger than the diameter of your faceplate. The block should be thick enough to hold the screws that will attach it to the faceplate. Fasten the block to the faceplate, then spread an even coating of yellow glue on the block and center it on the bowl blank. Use two clamps to secure the pieces together with even pressure and allow the adhesive to cure. Once the turning is done, the glue block can be parted off from the blank.

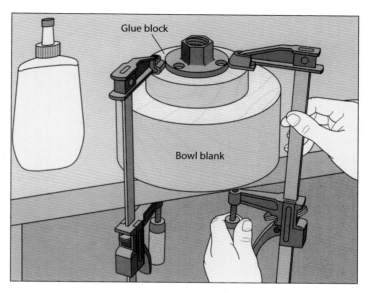

Glue block

Bowl blank

Paper Joints

Assembling the joint

The paper joint is identical to the glue block method described above, except that a sheet of kraft paper is sandwiched between the glue block and the bowl blank. The paper allows the pieces to be pried apart once the bowl is turned. Screw the faceplate to the glue block, ensuring the screws do not pass through the block. Then spread a thin layer of glue on the bottom of the bowl blank and on the glue block. Place a piece of kraft paper slightly larger than the glue block on the workpiece, set the glue block on the paper *(left)*, then clamp the assembly as you would a glue joint.

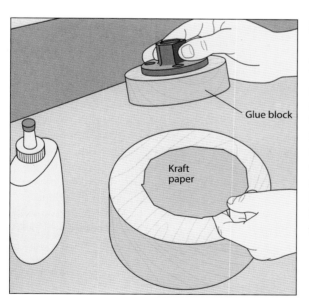

Glue block

Kraft paper

Attaching a Blank with Double-Sided Tape

Applying the tape

Double-sided turning tape provides a simple way to secure a lightweight blank for faceplate turning. Cut strips of two-sided turning tape to cover as much of the faceplate as possible. Remove the backing paper from one side of the strips and fix them on the faceplate. Then, peel the paper off the other side of the tape *(right)*. Press the faceplate on the blank, centering it as well as possible on the stock.

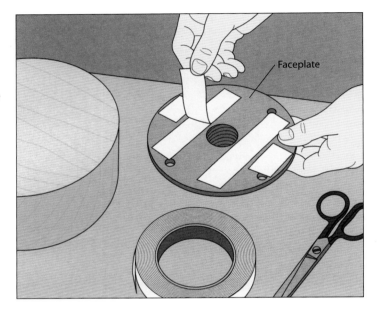

Faceplate

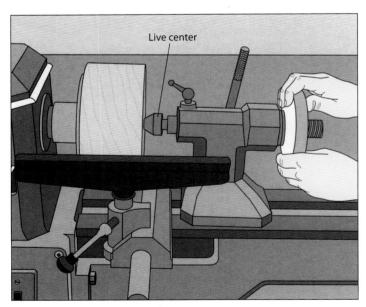

Live center

Mounting the assembly on the lathe

Use pressure from the tailstock to reinforce the tape bond between the faceplate and the turning blank. Install the faceplate on the headstock spindle. Then insert a live center in the tailstock and slide it against the blank. Turn the hand-wheel to increase the pressure *(left)*. You can now either move the tailstock away from the blank and shape the outside of the bowl or leave the tailstock in place. Do not leave the blank on the lathe for an extended time, as gravity will loosen the holding power of the tape; instead, when you stop work remove the faceplate from the headstock and set the assembly down flat.

Two Centering Jigs

Making and using a faceplate-centering jig

To center your lathe's faceplate on a circular blank, use the jig shown at right. Turn a piece of wood into a cylinder the same diameter as the faceplate's threaded hole, tapering the end slightly. (You may wish to form a handle at the top of the jig.) Drive a nail into the center of the tapered end, cut off the nail head, and grind a sharp point. To use the jig, mark the center of the blank with an awl and set the faceplate on the workpiece with the mark in the middle of the threaded hole. Insert the jig in the hole *(right)*, and "feel" for the mark with the nail tip. Holding the jig in place, screw the faceplate to the blank.

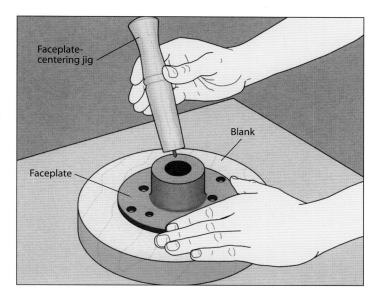

Faceplate-centering jig

Blank

Faceplate

Acrylic plastic disk

Skew chisel

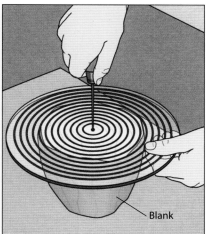

Blank

Making and using a center-finding jig

The jig shown above will enable you to center a faceplate on an irregularly shaped blank. Cut pieces of ¼-inch clear acrylic plastic and ¾-inch plywood into 12-inch-diameter disks. Leaving the paper backing on both sides of the plastic, attach the two together with double-sided tape and a central screw. Mount them to your faceplate so the plastic is facing out. Use a skew chisel to cut a series of equally spaced, concentric rings in the disk *(above, left)*. Remove the plastic from the plywood and spray it with black paint. Once the paint has dried, peel the backing paper off both sides of the plastic. To use the jig, position the blank so as much of it as possible is within one of the rings and mark the center with an awl *(above, right)*.

Scroll Chucks (Contracting Jaws)

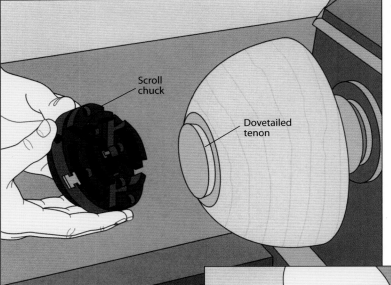

Attaching the chuck to a blank

Scroll chucks are attached to the base of a bowl blank after the outside of the blank has been shaped *(page 100)*. For a chuck with contracting jaws, you will also need to turn a dovetailed tenon on the bottom of the blank. (Follow the manufacturer's instructions for the appropriate size of the tenon.) Adjust the jaws of the chuck so they will slip over the tenon *(left)*. Hand-tighten the jaws around the tenon by turning the scroll ring, then remove the blank from the lathe and unscrew the faceplate.

Tightening the chuck jaws

Thread the chuck onto the headstock of your lathe, then finish tightening the chuck jaws around the tenon following the manufacturer's instructions. For the model shown, you must tighten the chuck scroll ring while holding the chuck body stationary. If your lathe has a spindle lock, hold the spindle steady with it and use the scroll lever to tighten the scroll ring. If your machine has no spindle lock, use the body handle to hold the chuck body as you tighten the scroll ring *(right)*.

Scroll Chucks (Expanding Jaws)

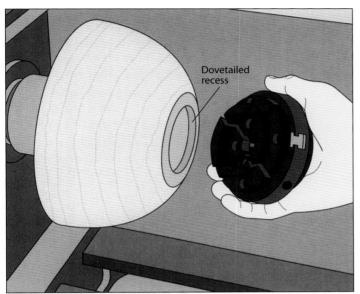

Dovetailed recess

Fitting the chuck in the recess

To attach a scroll chuck with expanding jaws to a bowl blank, you must first turn a dovetailed recess in the bottom of the bowl to suit the jaws *(page 103)*. (Follow the manufacturer's instructions for the size of the recess.) Then fit the jaws into the recess *(left)* and turn the scroll ring by hand to secure the chuck. Remove the blank from the lathe and unscrew the faceplate.

Tightening the chuck

Set the blank face down on a work surface and tighten the jaws in the recess following the manufacturer's instructions. For the model shown, insert the scroll lever in the scroll ring and the body handle in the chuck body *(below)*, and tighten the ring and body against each other until the jaws grip the walls of the recess tightly.

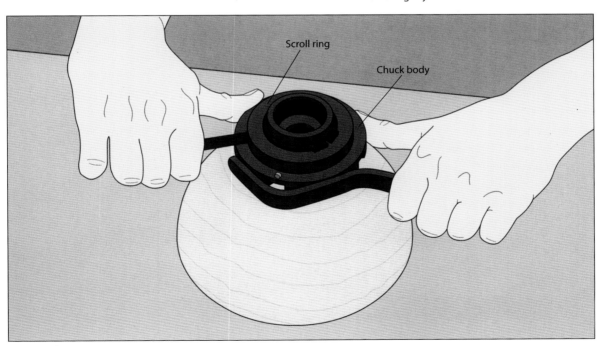

Scroll ring

Chuck body

Faceplate Turning

Back to **Basics**

91

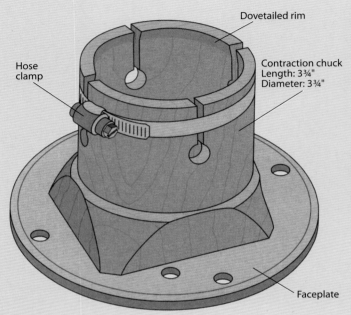

Dovetailed rim

Hose
clamp

Contraction chuck
Length: 3¾"
Diameter: 3¾"

Faceplate

A Contraction Chuck

The contraction chuck shown at left can be fashioned from a small block of wood. The dimensions in the illustration will enable the jig to secure the bottom of a large-sized goblet blank to the lathe headstock.

To make the jig, mount a blank on the headstock and turn it to a cylinder. Then use a round-nose scraper to hollow out a recess about 1¼ inch deep in the center of the cylinder (below, left). Follow the

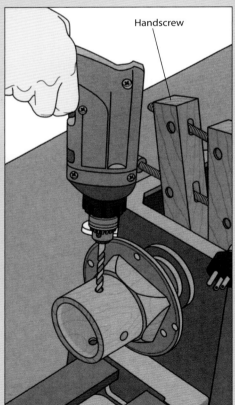

Handscrew

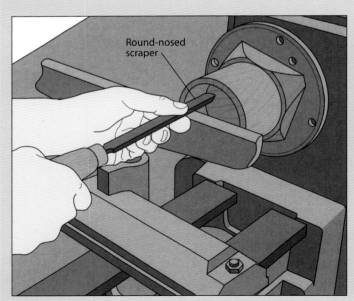

Round-nosed
scraper

same procedure as you would to hollow out a goblet *(page 122)*, leaving the walls of the chuck about ¼ inch thick. Then use a side-cutting scraper to remove additional wood just below the top edge of the rim, creating a dovetailed lip around the inside edge. This will mesh with a dovetailed tenon you will turn in the bottom of your workpiece, helping to hold it in the chuck. Make sure you brace each scraper on the tool rest as you make these cuts.

Now, bore four ⅜ -inch holes around the circumference, spaced 90° apart and located 1¼ inch below the rim of the chuck, flush with the bottom of the recess. For the

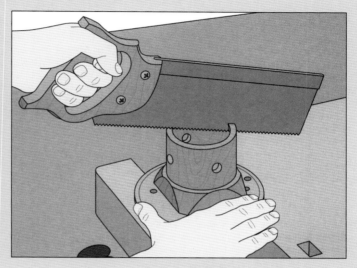

first hole, clamp the drive shaft with a handscrew to prevent the spindle from rotating. To drill the remaining holes, remove the hand-screw, rotate the chuck 90°, and clamp the drive shaft again *(facing page, bottom right)*. Now remove the faceplate from the headstock and secure it in a vise. Use a handsaw to cut four kerfs from the rim into the holes that you drilled *(above)*. These cuts will define the jaws of your chuck. Widen the kerfs to ⅛ inch using a chisel, then install a hose clamp around the chuck.

To use the chuck, turn a dovetailed tenon on your workpiece slightly smaller than the diameter of the recess in the jig, mount the chuck and faceplate on the lathe headstock, and insert the workpiece in the chuck *(left)*. Tighten the hose clamp to secure the stock in place.

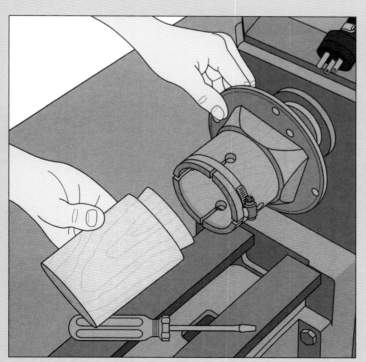

Screw Chucks

Preparing the blank

The screw chuck is easy to use, but it is not strong enough to hold large blanks or secure end grain. Refer to the manufacturer's instructions for limitations on the size of blanks you can use. For the model shown below, a maximum diameter-to-length ratio of 3:1 is recommended. Additional support can be provided for large blanks by sliding the tailstock against the work as you turn the bowl. To prepare your blank for the screw chuck, plane the contacting face of the blank so the chuck's collar will fit flush against it. Bore a pilot hole into the center of the blank to accommodate the chuck screw *(right)*—in this case, a ¼-inch hole to a depth of 1 inch.

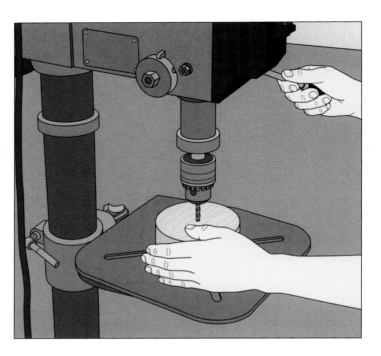

Mounting the blank

Screw the chuck to the headstock spindle of the lathe, then attach the blank to the chuck *(below)*. Screw on the blank until it sits firmly against the screw collar.

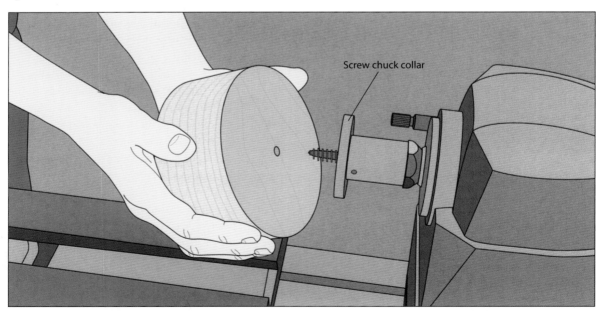

Screw chuck collar

Jacobs Chuck

Although the Jacobs chuck, like the one shown in the photo at left, is normally used in the tailstock to hold drill bits for hollowing, it is also ideal for securing small-diameter blanks to the headstock. Here, the chuck holds a chess piece made of tulipwood.

Three-Way Split-Ring Chucks

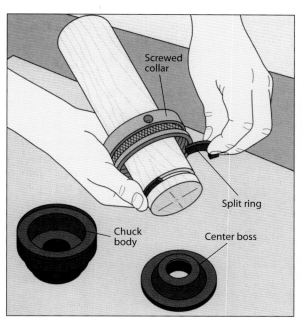

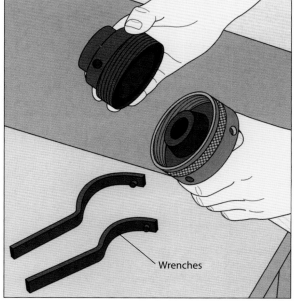

Attaching the chuck to a blank
The three-way split ring chuck is ideal for securing small goblet blanks and other pieces whose grain runs the length of the piece. Prepare your blank following the manufacturer's instructions. For the model shown, you need to turn the piece to a diameter of 2½ inches. Then use a parting tool to cut a ⅜-inch-square groove around the stock, ⅜ inch from the headstock-end. The groove will accommodate the split rings of the chuck. Remove the blank from the lathe, slide the threaded collar over the blank, and insert the split rings into the groove, ensuring that the sloping faces of the rings face toward the collar *(above, left)*. Assemble the chuck by placing the center boss against the threaded collar with the tapered end facing out, then screw the chuck body to the threaded collar *(above, right)*. Tighten the unit using the wrenches supplied with the chuck. This will lock the blank in place. Finally, screw the assembly onto the lathe's headstock spindle.

Pin Chucks

Setting up the chuck

The pin chuck allows you to mount a bowl blank on the lathe headstock quickly at the cost of drilling a relatively large hole in your workpiece. The chuck consists of two parts: a shaft with a flat wedge milled out of it and a roller pin that fits into the wedge. As shown in the illustration at right, when the pin is positioned in the middle of the wedge it is flush with the circumference of the shaft. This enables you to slip your blank over the chuck. Then, when you rotate the blank by hand, the pin rolls over to one side and protrudes slightly above the top of the shaft, wedging the blank to the headstock. To set up the chuck, simply thread it on the headstock, rotate it so the wedge is facing up and place the roller pin in the middle of the wedge.

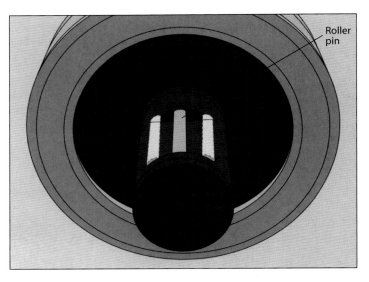

Roller pin

Roller pin

Preparing and mounting the blank

Prepare your stock for the pin chuck following the manufacturer's instructions. For the model shown, bore a 1-inch-diameter hole into the blank deep enough so the full length of the pin can penetrate the piece. As you will be using the pin chuck to turn the outside of the bowl, be sure to drill the hole into the part that will be hollowed out later. Slide the blank on the chuck (*left*), then turn the blank by hand against the direction of headstock rotation until the roller pin locks the workpiece in place.

Collet Chucks

Mounting a bowl blank

Once you have shaped the outside of your blank, a collet chuck will enable you to attach the bottom to the headstock of the lathe for hollowing out the inside. This chuck is similar in operation to the contracting-jaw scroll chuck described on page 90. To prepare a blank for the chuck, turn a dovetailed tenon on the bottom. (Follow the manufacturer's instructions for the appropriate size of the tenon.) For the model shown, the tenon should be slightly smaller in diameter than the chuck's collet when it is opened. (You may remove the tenon once the inside of the bowl is turned.) Next, install the chuck on the headstock spindle, insert the tenon in the collet, and tighten the threaded collar—first by hand, then using the wrenches supplied with the chuck.

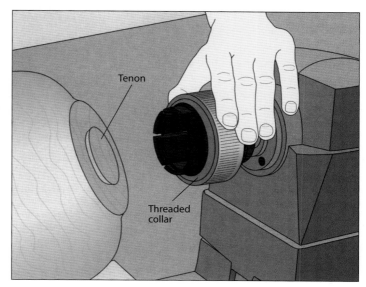

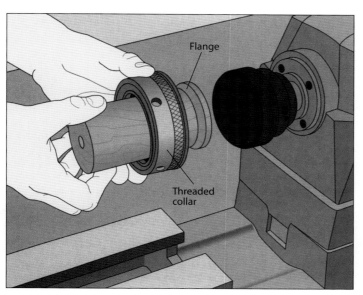

Collar Chucks

Mounting the workpiece

The collar chuck allows you to secure goblets and other long blanks on the lathe's headstock without using the tailstock. Prepare your stock and assemble the chuck following the manufacturer's instructions. For the model shown, start by mounting it between centers, then turn it into a cylinder with a diameter of 2½ inches, with a ½-inch-long sloping flange, or collar, at the headstock end of the workpiece. The diameter of the flange should be at least 2¾ inches. Once the blank is ready, remove it from the lathe and slide the threaded collar onto it, making certain that the sloping face of the flange faces the collar *(left)*. Finally, tighten the collar on the chuck body using the wrenches provided with the chuck.

Faceplate Turning

Back to Basics

97

Bowl Turning

There is no single way to turn a bowl. As you gain experience faceplate turning, you will develop a technique that works best for you and the sort of work you do. This section of the chapter traces three bowl-turning projects from start to finish, including two conventional bowls and a natural-top bowl made from green wood.

The bowl gouge is the workhorse of bowl turning. As shown below, you must always try to keep the gouge's bevel rubbing lightly on the blank as it cuts. This provides support for the cutting edge and controls the depth of cut.

Depending on the shape of your blank, this may be difficult as you start to turn a bowl. Set the lathe to its lowest speed until you have rounded the blank to a disk. A gouge cuts most smoothly when the cutting edge is slightly over on its side so that the flute is facing the direction of the cut.

Scraping tools are also used extensively in bowl turning. For roughing out waste, the blade must lie flat on the tool rest *(page 103)*.

The direction of cut is also critical. Because the grain of faceplate work runs at a right angle to the lathe axis, your cutting will run against the grain as well as with it. As much as possible when turning the outside of a bowl,

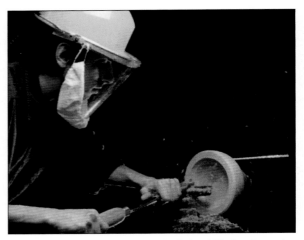

A bowl gouge hollows out the mouth of a bowl. The hood worn by the turner is hooked up by a hose to a small, belt-mounted pump and filter that provide a steady stream of fresh air. The clear plastic shield provides protection from flying debris.

cuts should run from small diameter to large, or from the bottom of the bowl to the top. Inside work should be performed from the rim to the bottom.

Correct Body and Tool Position

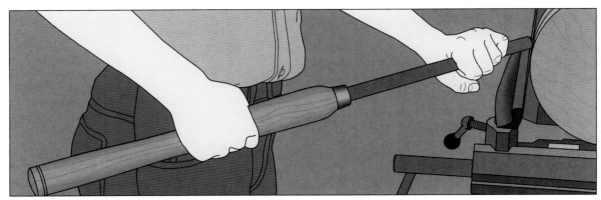

Maintaining your stance and gripping the tool
Stand close to the lathe, with your feet a comfortable distance apart. Grasp the tool in both hands: Hold the middle of the handle with your right hand; with your left hand, grip the blade near the tip and press it down firmly on the tool rest. Tool movements are generated by shifting your body in a controlled manner. Simply moving your arms and hands will tend to make the tool swing in an arc and reduce your control.

Incorrect cutting technique

Touching a bowl gouge to a spinning blank without the bevel rubbing *(right)* is dangerous for you and damaging for your workpiece. With the cutting edge in this position, the cut is virtually impossible to control. You run the risk of digging the cutting edge into the piece. This can produce unsightly notches in your stock and cause you to lose control of the tool. Another mistake is pushing the cutting edge against the wood before the tool contacts the tool rest. This will invariably slam the blade against the tool rest with a force that could damage the work, the tool rest, or the gouge.

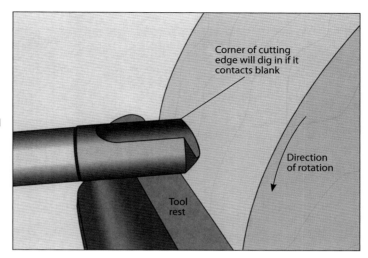

Corner of cutting edge will dig in if it contacts blank

Direction of rotation

Tool rest

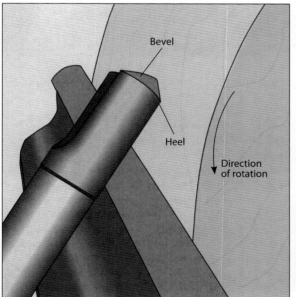

Bevel

Heel

Direction of rotation

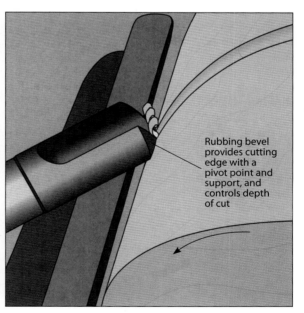

Rubbing bevel provides cutting edge with a pivot point and support, and controls depth of cut

Correct cutting technique

Brace the blade on the tool rest before it contacts the wood. Then, with the handle held low, advance the tool toward the spinning blank until the heel of the bevel is rubbing against the wood *(above, left)*. To begin cutting, gradually lift the handle, bringing the cutting edge in contact with the stock and the bevel flush against the wood *(above, right)*. Keep in mind that the tool will travel in the direction that the flute is pointed.

Rounding a Blank

Using a bowl gouge

Mount the blank on the lathe headstock and position the tool rest ¼ inch from the stock. Rotate the blank by hand to ensure that it does not contact the rest, then turn on the lathe. Bracing the gouge on the tool rest at one edge of the piece, advance the blade until the heel of the bevel contacts the stock. Then pivot up the handle until the cutting edge begins slicing into the wood. Roll the gouge so that the flute is facing the direction of the cut—in this case, toward the headstock-end of the lathe—and move the tool along the blank to remove a thin layer of wood *(right)*. Continue in this manner until the diameter of the blank is slightly greater than the finished bowl diameter. Once the shape is satisfactory and the bowl is the proper diameter, flatten the face *(page 105)* before shaping the outside.

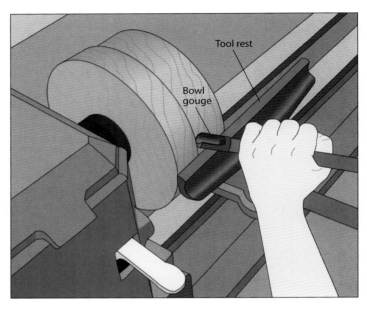

Tool rest

Bowl gouge

Shaping the Outside of the Bowl

Rounding the corner of the blank

Position the tool rest ¼ inch from the corner of the blank and angled at roughly 45° to the bottom. Adjust the height of the rest so it is level with the center of the blank. Set the gouge on the right-hand side of the tool rest with the flute pointing in the direction of the cut. Starting on the bottom of the bowl about 1 inch from the corner of the blank, advance the tool until the bevel rubs on the stock. Pivot the tool handle up until the edge is cutting, then move the tool to the left to chamfer the corner *(left)*. Continue, cutting from the center outward to the edges to round the corner of the blank. Move the tool rest periodically to keep it as close as possible to the blank.

Rounding the outside of the blank

Continue working from the center toward the rim of the blank (from smaller to larger diameter) to shape the outside of the bowl to the desired diameter and curve. Reposition the tool rest as necessary to follow the curve of the bowl. Always brace the gouge on the tool rest, making certain that the flute faces the direction of the cut—from the bottom to the top of the bowl. As shown at right, you will need to pivot the handle and roll the blade to keep the bevel rubbing on the stock.

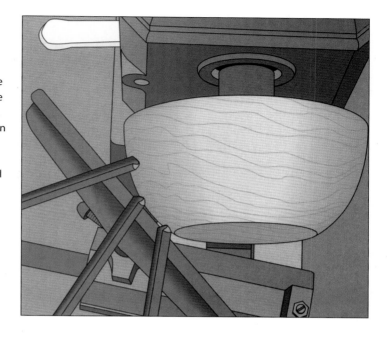

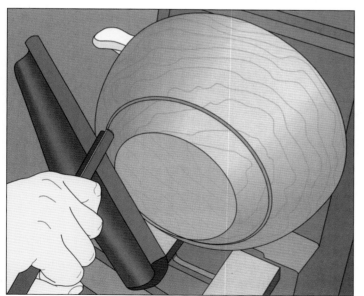

Final shaping

Refine the shape of the bowl with the bowl gouge, adding design elements such as concave curves or decorative grooves at this time. Keep the flute pointing in the direction of the cut and the bevel rubbing on the wood *(left)*. Remember to account for the method you will use to chuck the bottom of the bowl to the headstock to hollow out the inside. If you will be turning a dovetailed recess for an expanding jaw chuck *(page 103)*, as on the blank shown, leave the bottom flat and large enough for the recess.

Faceplate Turning

Back to **Basics**

101

Flattening the Bottom

Bowl gouge

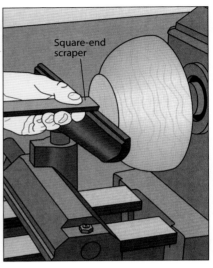

Square-end
scraper

Flattening the base

Once you have shaped the outside of the bowl, it is time to reverse the blank by attaching the base to the lathe headstock so you can hollow out the vessel. If you will be using a glue block, first flatten the base with a bowl gouge or square-end scraper. If you will be using a chuck, you can prepare the base of the bowl for it *(page 103)*. To flatten the base, position the tool rest parallel to the base. Tilt the gouge's handle down a little and cut from the outside toward the center *(above, left)*, removing wood in thin layers until the base is flat. If you are using a scraper, angle the handle up slightly so the burr on the cutting edge is shaving wood from the base *(above, right)*.

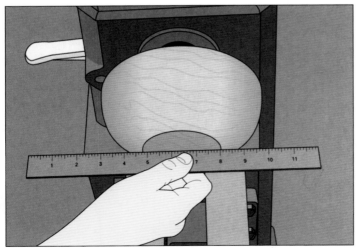

Checking for flatness

Periodically use a straightedge, such as a rule, to check whether the bottom is flat. Hold the rule on edge against the base *(left)* and look for any gaps.

Preparing the Base for a Chuck

Cutting the recess

If you will be using a chuck that calls for a dovetailed recess in the base, as on the bowl illustrated on this page, use a side-cutting skew scraper to form the recess. The cavity should be sized to fit the jaws of the chuck; you can use dividers to mark the required diameter on the base. Then position the tool rest slightly below the center of the base so that the scraper's edge will lie at the centerline. Hold the scraper blade flat on the rest and, with the handle lifted up slightly, advance the tool to the left of the center until the burr contacts the blank. Cut the recess slowly to the depth specified by the chuck manufacturer. Then slide the scraper to the edge of the cavity and cut the dovetail in the wall of the recess *(right)*. Keep the blade flat on the tool rest throughout the operation.

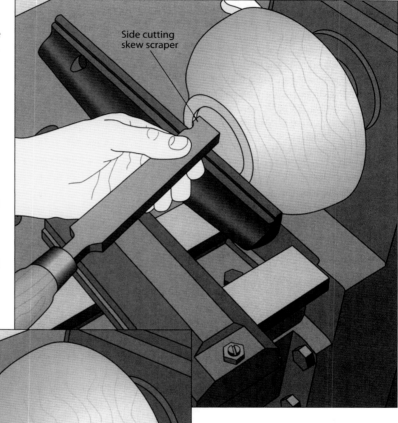

Side cutting skew scraper

Chuck jaws

Checking the recess

When you have completed the recess, assemble the jaws of the chuck, using an elastic band to hold them together, and fit the jaws in place to check the fit *(left)*. The jaws should go all the way in with a small amount of clearance. Deepen or widen the recess if necessary.

Finishing the Outside of the Bowl

Smoothing the surface

Although a gouge leaves the outside of the bowl relatively uniform, it may also leave a few ripples. Dragging a scraper very lightly across the surface will clean up the surface. This operation is known as "shear scraping." Position the tool rest parallel to the outside of the bowl and turn on the lathe. Hold a freshly sharpened round-nosed scraper with one corner of the blade contacting the tool rest, as shown at right. Starting at the bottom of the bowl, drag the cutting edge lightly and smoothly along the outside of the bowl, working from the base towards the rim. The cut should produce fine shavings. Repeat the cut as often as necessary until you produce the finish you want.

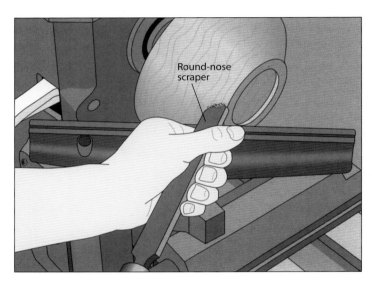

Round-nose scraper

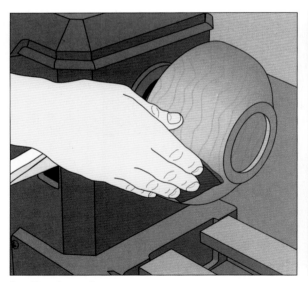

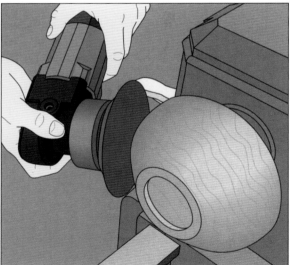

Sanding the surface

The final step before hollowing out the inside of a bowl is sanding the outside. You can either work by hand or use a random-orbit sander. In either case, move the lathe's tool rest out of the way. If you are working by hand, fold the sandpaper twice, turn on the lathe, and hold the paper lightly against the blank.

Keep the paper below the middle of the bowl *(above, left)* and move the pad from the base to the rim of the bowl to cover the entire surface. With the power sander, work the same way, holding the sanding disk lightly against the surface *(above, right)*. Start with 100-grit paper and move to progressively finer grits.

Hollowing out the Bowl

Once you have turned the outside of a bowl, it is time to hollow it out. Your approach here is critical to the ultimate appearance of the piece. Keep in mind that the shape of a bowl's inside should complement the outside. A bowl can have attractive outside and inside forms, but if the surfaces do not harmonize, the finished piece will not look right. As a novice bowl turner, you should aim for walls of even thickness. For small- to medium-sized bowls, ⅛-to ¼-inch-thick walls work well. As you gain experience, do not hesitate to experiment with less conventional designs.

The most important rule when hollowing out is to cut toward the axis of the lathe—that is, from large to small diameter. The advantage of this approach is that your cuts will run with the grain, giving you better control of the tool and producing a cleaner surface.

For judging depth, many turners drill a depth hole into the mouth of the bowl before starting *(below)*. Although it is not absolutely necessary, a depth hole will allow you to work without stopping often to measure your progress.

Once you are ready to hollow out the interior, chuck the bowl base to the headstock using one of the methods described earlier in the chapter. Then flatten the face of

A crucial step before hollowing out the inside of a bowl is to flatten the face of the mouth. This will ensure that the distance between the rim and the base is uniform all around the circumference.

the mouth, as shown in the photo above. To prevent the rim from splintering, touch it lightly with a bowl gouge to round it over slightly. Now you are ready to rough out the inside. Once you have removed the bulk of the waste and the inside of the bowl has the rough form you want, use a scraper to refine the surface. These procedures are shown in the following pages.

Remember that on large bowls, there will be times when the tool's pivot point on the tool rest will be relatively far from the cut. In such cases, brace the cutting tool firmly on the rest and work carefully.

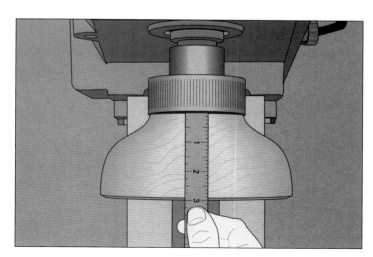

Turning the Inside of the Bowl

Measuring the depth of the bowl

Before you begin hollowing the bowl, measure the depth of the blank to determine how far you can cut into the mouth before you will reach the chuck recess or faceplate screws. Holding a rule directly above the blank, measure from the mouth to the base *(left)*. The bowl shown in the illustration is secured to the lathe headstock with a chuck. Subtract the depth of the recess for the chuck (in this case, ¼ inch) and the eventual thickness of the base (about ¼ inch) to arrive at the depth to which you can cut (for the bowl shown, 2¼ inches).

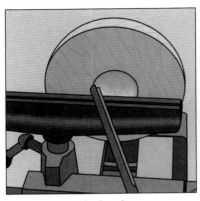 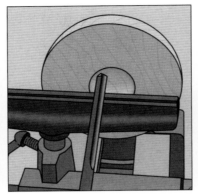 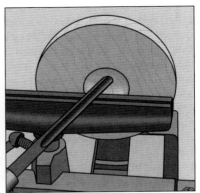

Hollowing out the bowl

Position the tool rest so the gouge tip will cut slightly above the middle of the blank. Turn on the lathe and align the cutting edge just to the left of the center of the blank. Then, with the gouge on its side and the flute facing the center of the piece, push the tool slowly into the blank. For the first ⅛ inch, the bevel will not be rubbing against the wood. Once it begins to rub, guide the cutting edge to the center of the blank. Continue the process, forming a shallow cavity in the middle of the mouth. As the cavity becomes larger, pivot the handle from side to side in a shallow arc, as shown above, pushing the cutting edge against the side of the hole until it reaches the center. (The hands have been removed from the illustration for clarity.) Support the blade as you would to shape the outside (page 98). Turn the inside of the bowl to match the outside, but leave the walls a little thicker than you need. You will reach your final thickness later. As you approach your final depth, it may be difficult to make one fluid cut along the inside wall of the bowl. If so, you can make a series of shorter cuts from the rim to the center.

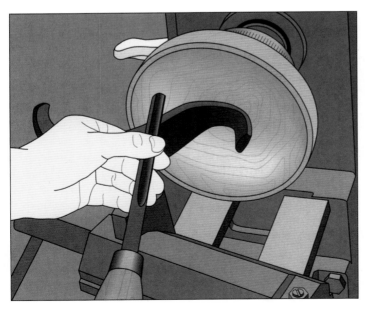

Finishing the inside

As the depth of bowl increases, you need to angle the tool rest so that it remains roughly parallel to the surface you are cutting. Or, you can turn off the lathe, remove the standard tool rest, and install an S-shaped rest. Position it so that part of the "S" is inside the bowl and roughly follows its curvature. Turn on the lathe again. Starting at the rim, make a light cut to trim the walls to the desired thickness. With the gouge pivoted well to the right, advance the tool into the cut and swing the handle to the left, keeping the bevel rubbing at all times. This technique will yield a smooth curve on the inside of the bowl. To obtain uniform wall thickness from the rim to the bottom, keep the bevel aligned with the outside profile of the bowl throughout the cut. Adjust the tool rest to keep it as close as possible to the inside surface of the bowl. Periodically measure wall thickness.

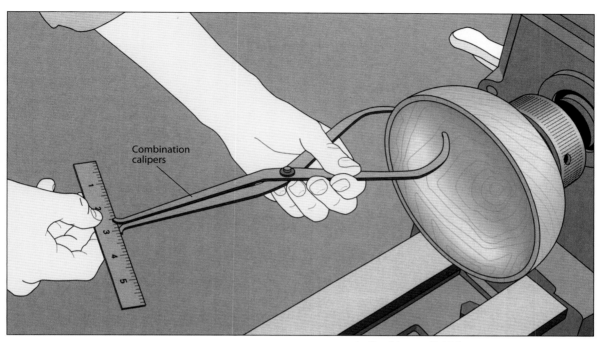

Combination
calipers

Shop Tip

Making a depth hole
One way to make certain that you hollow a bowl to the
correct depth is to drill a hole into the mouth to the
desired depth. With the blank mounted on the
lathe, install a Jacobs chuck and a twist or
brad-point bit in the tailstock. Mark the
desired depth on the bit
with a piece of masking
tape, then turn on the
lathe. Slide the tail stock
toward the blank until
the bit starts cutting.
Advance the tailstock
until the masking tape
contacts the blank.

Checking wall thickness
At the start of the hollowing out process, you
can gauge the wall thickness with your hands.
But as you approach your final thickness, use
combination calipers for a more precise reading.
Close one end of the calipers around the bowl
near the top and bottom and measure the
opening at the other end to determine the
thickness of the wall *(above)*. Continue finishing
the inside until the thickness is uniform.

Depth Gauge

Use the shop-made gauge shown below to check the depth of your bowl as you hollow it out. The jig is easy to build from scrap wood and ¼-inch dowel. Make the crossbar two or three times longer than the diameter of the largest bowl you can turn on your lathe. Cut it to the shape shown for a convenient grip.

To insert the measuring pin and wedge dowels, bore one hole from edge to edge through the middle of the crossbar and a second hole through from the top. The wedge hole should overlap the pin hole slightly so that the wedge will hold the pin in place. Drill both holes with a ¼-inch bit. Cut a long dowel for the measuring pin and round over its bowl-end with sandpaper to prevent the tip from scratching the inside of the bowl. Mark depth intervals on the pin using a ruler and a pencil. Next, cut a shorter dowel for the wedge and taper its bottom end.

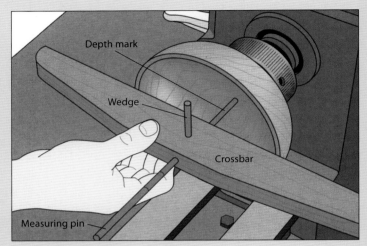

To use the jig, insert the measuring pin into its hole in the crossbar, then insert the wedge to lock the pin at the desired depth. Check your progress as you hollow out the bowl. The inside is at the correct depth when the measuring pin contacts the bottom of the bowl and the flat edge of the crossbar butts against the rim of the bowl.

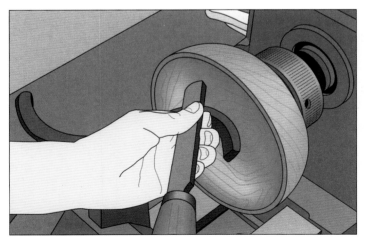

Smoothing the interior

Use a round-nosed scraper to shear-scrape the inside of the bowl before sanding. To avoid digging the blade into the wood, the curvature of the cutting edge must be tighter than the curve of the bowl's interior. Adjust the S-shaped tool rest so it roughly follows the inside of the bowl. Then, raising the scraper handle so the burr is even with the center of the bowl, press the scraper lightly against the inside of the bowl. With the blade at a 45° angle to the axis of the bowl, drag the blade gently over the entire interior surface, working from the bottom of the bowl to the rim until you obtain the desired smoothness *(left)*.

Sanding the inside of the bowl by hand

Fold a piece of 100-grit sandpaper and move the lathe's tool rest out of the way. Turn on the lathe, and hold the paper lightly against the inside surface of the bowl. Keep the paper below the midline of the bowl *(right)* and move the pad from the bottom to the rim to smooth the entire surface. Continue the process with a series of finer-grit papers.

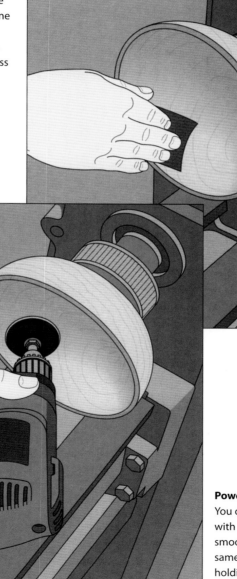

Power sanding the inside of the bowl

You can also use an electric drill fitted with an accessory sanding disk to smooth the inside of the bowl. Work the same way as you would with sandpaper, holding the sanding disk lightly against the surface *(left)*.

Applying a finish

With the bowl still on the lathe, saturate a rag or sponge with tung oil (varnish or lacquer may also be used), or a food-safe finish if the bowl will hold food, and run the machine at its slowest speed. Starting with the outside of the bowl, hold the rag lightly against the surface *(left)*, moving from the base to the rim. Use a clean, dry, lint-free rag to wipe off any excess finish. Then saturate the rag again and apply another coat to the inside of the bowl. Once the finish has dried, sand the bowl with 400-grit paper and wipe it clean. Apply several coats the same way, sanding between applications. With more coats, the bowl will better resist cracking and damage from heat and water.

Pumice powder

Polishing the finish

Once the final coat is dry, use pumice powder to polish it. Spread a dab of paste wax on a rag, then shake on a small amount of the powder. Run the lathe at its slowest speed and hold the rag against the inside and outside surfaces. Continue until the finish is silky smooth. Repeat the process with rottenstone, which is a fine abrasive powder.

Turning a Bowl with a Glue Block

Initial shaping

If you are using a glue block and a faceplate to turn a bowl, rather than a faceplate and a chuck, you can shape both the outside and inside with a single setup. Attach a faceplate and glue block to your blank *(page 87)*, then mount the faceplate to the lathe. Angle the tool rest so that it is roughly parallel to the final shape of the bowl's outside. Start turning the bowl by rounding its bottom edge with a gouge *(right)*. Brace the gouge on the tool rest with the flute pointing in the direction of the cut; keep the bevel rubbing at all times. Continue the cut to turn the outside of the bowl roughly to shape. Cut with the grain—from the base to the rim— as much as possible.

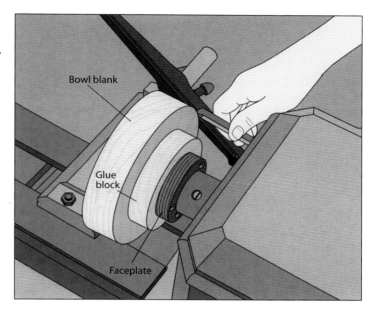

Bowl blank

Glue block

Faceplate

Finishing the bowl's outside shape

Once the outside shape of the bowl is satisfactory, use the gouge to make a series of fine, light cuts *(left)*, producing a smooth surface. Then hollow out the inside as you would using a chuck *(page 105)*. Sand and finish the bowl following the procedures shown on page 109.

Mouth of bowl

Parting off the bowl

Bracing a parting tool on the tool rest, advance it until the bevel is rubbing on the glue block, then pivot the cutting edge down to start the cut. Rotate the tool back and forth slightly so the blade will not bind *(right)*. Continue until only a small bridge of wood connects the bowl to the glue block. Then turn off the lathe and use a handsaw to cut the bridge and remove the bowl.

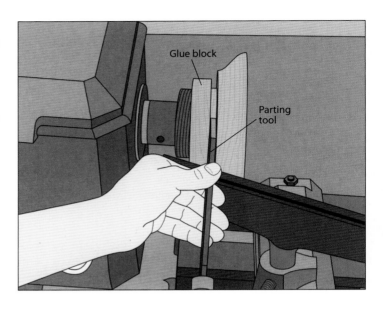

Glue block

Parting tool

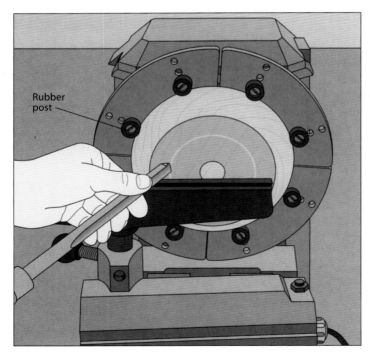

Rubber post

Cleaning up the bottom

The final step in the process involves turning the base of the bowl to follow the contour of the inside, making it slightly concave. You will also use a bowl gouge to remove any traces of the glue joint and parting cut. Attach the bowl to the lathe with a chuck, as shown at right. The model shown features four large adjustable jaws connected to a commercial scroll chuck. Rubber posts are inserted in the holes in the jaws to secure the bowl snugly. The posts must be located in the same hole in each of the jaw segments to ensure even pressure is applied to the bowl rim. Set up the chuck following the manufacturer's instructions, mount it on the headstock spindle of the lathe, then hold the bowl in the rubber posts and tighten the chuck. Do not overtighten, as this could damage the rim. Position the tool rest to cut the base of the bowl, then make a light cut across the base with the bevel rubbing and the flute facing the direction of the cut *(left)*.

Natural-Top Bowls

As the esthetic emphasis in wood turning has shifted over the last 30 years from the utilitarian to the decorative, turners have begun to explore new designs. Natural-top bowls, which follow the outside curve of a log at the rim, are an example of this experimentation and the recent efforts of turners to highlight the natural characteristics of wood. The bark can be left on the rim, as in the example shown at right, or removed. The steps needed to turn such a piece are shown in the following pages.

Natural-top bowls often are given relatively simple shapes, emphasizing the grain pattern and shape of a particular log. Ash, apple, cherry, oak, and maple are all good choices for raw materials, but you do not need to limit yourself to just these few types of wood. Experiment with what is available and you may be pleasantly surprised by the results.

The drying process can cause some problems with your workpieces. If your wood is green, or wet, the bowl will be easy to turn, but regardless of how carefully the piece is dried, it will warp, perhaps substantially. You should try to turn the log into a bowl within an hour of cutting, before the piece dries and becomes distorted. An advantage of this process is that bark adheres better to green wood. In addition, the piece may warp into a unique and attractive shape.

If you want to minimize warping, dry your stock before turning it. With dense woods, it is best to turn the wood into a rough bowl blank when it is still green to ensure that the piece dries evenly and to help prevent it from cracking. This method is shown starting below.

The raw quality of a natural-top bowl belies the fact that it is often carefully crafted. In the example shown in the photo above, wood turner Betty Scarpino has left the bark on the rim as a visual reminder of the bowl in its original form—a fresh log.

A microwave oven can speed the drying process: Using the "defrost" setting, put the piece through several brief cycles of heating and cooling until it is dry. If you air-dry the stock, put it in a plastic bag or coat it with wax to prevent too-rapid drying, which will cause the wood to crack. If you use a bag, turn it inside out periodically to prevent mold from forming. It can take several weeks for a rough-hewn blank to air dry.

Making a Natural-Top Bowl

Planning the process

Once you have selected a log for your bowl, saw it into blocks and examine the end grain. Choose the half of one of the pieces that will yield the most attractive bowl. Use a piece of chalk or a lumber crayon to outline the bowl on the end of the log, locating the base at the pith and the rim at the bark. Then draw a line across the center at the base of the bowl outline. Saw the log in half along this line.

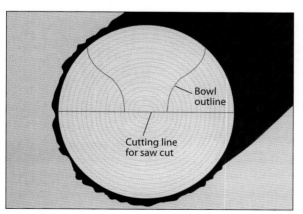

Bowl outline

Cutting line for saw cut

Preparing the blank

Cut your half-log to length, making it about 2 inches longer than the desired diameter of the bowl. Then prepare the blank for the lathe by cutting it into a circle on the band saw. Set the blank bark-side up on the saw table and adjust the upper guide assembly ⅛ inch above the blank's highest point. Since the blank does not have to be a perfect circle, you can make this cut freehand, as shown at right. Make sure you feed the block with both hands, keeping them clear of the blade at all times. Another option is to cut a cardboard template into the circle you want and nail the template to the top of the blank. The saw blade will then be guided by the edge of the cardboard as you make the cut.

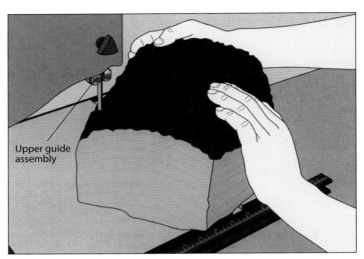

Upper guide assembly

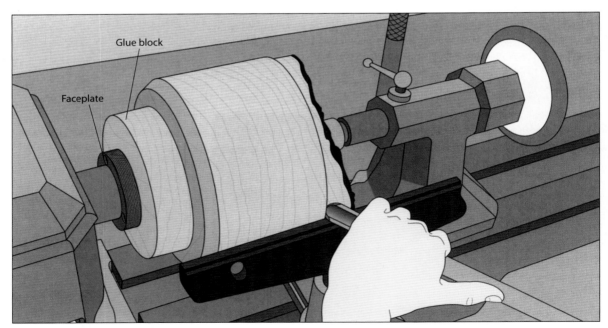

Glue block

Faceplate

Truing the blank

Mount the blank on the lathe headstock using a faceplate and a glue block *(page 87)*. Use cyanoacrylate glue with green wood. Install a live center in the tailstock and slide it against the piece to provide additional support as you turn the bowl. Position the tool rest beside the blank, turn on the lathe at its slowest speed, and use a bowl gouge to turn the stock into a smooth, cylindrical blank *(above)*. Lay the blade on the spinning blank to test its smoothness *(page 56)*.

Faceplate Turning

Rough-shaping the outside of the bowl blank

Use the bowl gouge to cut the bowl's outside to shape. Working from the base to the rim, or from small to large diameter, will help ensure a clean cut. Roll the flute in the direction of the cut and move the gouge along the tool rest *(right)*. Continue until you are satisfied with the shape of the blank, advancing the tool rest periodically to keep it close to the blank. Before refining the bowl's outside shape, you need to hollow out the inside and let the blank dry.

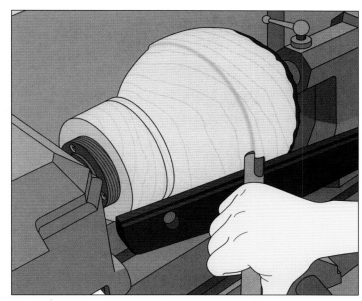

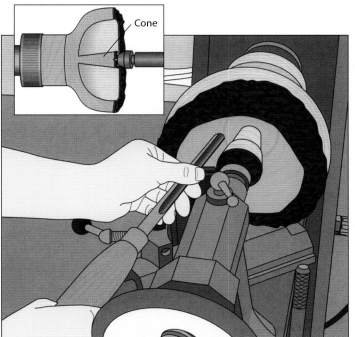

Cone

Hollowing the blank

Hollow out the blank with a bowl gouge, working beside the tailstock to cut as deeply as you can. With the cutting edge just to the left of the live center in the tailstock, cut increasingly deeper arcs to hollow out the bowl. Keep the blade braced on the tool rest, the bevel rubbing on the stock and the flute pointing in the direction of the cut *(left)*. Continue until the walls of the bowl are about 1½ inches thick; walls of even thickness will dry more uniformly than uneven walls. A cone of wood will be left between the bottom of the bowl and the tailstock *(inset)*; this will allow the tailstock to continue to support the blank. Leave the bark on the rim of the bowl. If a piece breaks off, you can glue it back on later. Once the blank has the shape you want, part the piece from the glue block *(page 112)*.

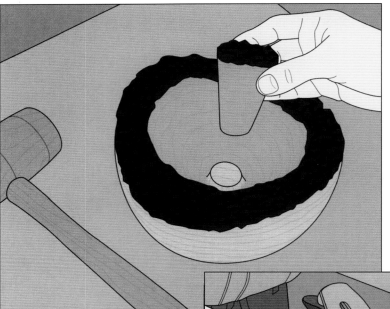

Removing the cone

Place the blank on a work surface and tap the cone lightly with a mallet to break it from the bottom of the bowl. Before continuing to shape the bowl, you need to let it dry. As described on page 113, you can shorten the drying time using a microwave oven, or let the blank air dry.

Flattening the base

The drying process will likely cause the blank to warp. The result is often oval in shape. You will need to plane the base flat and smooth before re-mounting it to a glue block to finish turning the bowl. Once the bowl has dried sufficiently, check the base for smoothness and flatness. If it is rough or warped, clamp it to a work surface and use a hand plane to correct the problem.

Smoothing the bowl

Mount the blank to the headstock using a faceplate and glue block. Use a bowl gouge to shape the bowl's exterior. Then use a square-end scraper to shear-scrape the outside surface of the blank. Position the tool rest along the side of the bowl. With the corner of the scraper bearing lightly on the rest, drag the burr gently along the blank, working from the base to the rim *(right)*. Continue until the outside of the bowl is smooth. Next, working from the blank's interior, use a bowl gouge to reduce the thickness of the walls to ¼ to ½ inch. Then smooth the inside of the bowl with a round-nose scraper *(page 108)*. Be careful during this stage not to slice the bark from the rim of the bowl. If a piece comes off, reattach it with thin cyanoacrylate glue.

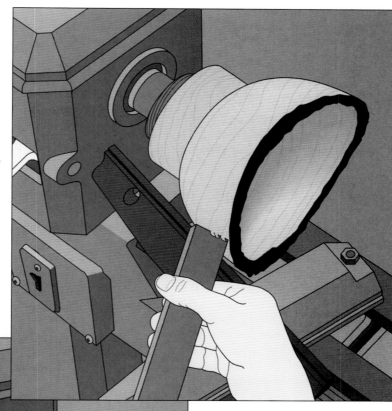

Sanding the bowl

Once you are satisfied with the shape of the bowl, sand the surface to the desired smoothness and apply a finish *(page 110)*. Finally, part the bowl from the glue block *(page 112)* and plane or sand the bottom smooth.

Turning Projects

Spindles and bowls are only two of a seemingly limitless variety of objects you can turn. Goblets, small pots used to display dried weeds or flowers (also known as weed pots), and boxes are popular turning projects. They can be made from a variety of solid woods, laminations—and even nuts and seed pods. These and other projects are described in this chapter.

Over the years, wood turners have devised dozens of ways to expand their repertoire. Some of these techniques involve how the blank is prepared or mounted on the lathe, rather than the turning process itself. In off-center turning, for example, standard turning skills are used; but because the piece is mounted off center, the finished product looks different from a standard spindle. Turning a cabriole leg with this technique is shown starting on page 120; steps for turning a tabletop are detailed on page 134.

Using veneer or contrasting wood inserts provides another way of enhancing a turned piece. Popularized by wood turner Dale Nish, this technique can be used to make laminated bowls *(page 136)* or plates *(page 138)*.

The techniques for turning goblets *(page 122)*, lidded boxes *(page 126)*, and weed pots *(page 131)* are not very different from those used to turn bowls. But in order to hollow out such vessels, you need to turn into end grain, which presents its own challenges. End-grain turning is much like spindle turning without the tailstock. Fruit-woods like persimmon and apple are excellent for this type of work, but any dense hardwood with fine, straight grain is suitable. Green wood also turns easily, but it will warp when it dries. To circumvent this problem, rough out the piece and then wait until it dries before turning it to its final shape. There is no need to spend much money on the wood needed for most of the projects shown in this chapter. Each can be made from small bits of leftover stock which might otherwise be discarded.

Designs and sizes for these pieces vary widely. Goblets can be turned to a simple cup shape. But as you gain experience, you may wish to try turning a tulip or trumpet flower form, both popular profiles. Because these pieces often have fragile walls and stems, complete each section as you go. Once a goblet is hollowed out, for example, sand and finish the inside while there is surrounding wood to support the bowl. If you wait until the whole piece is turned, you run the risk of breaking the stem or cracking the bowl.

Developed by Seattle wood turner Bonnie Klein, the Klein Design Miniature Lathe shown above is used for producing small-scale turnings. Used by amateur and professional turners alike, the lathe is driven by a ¼-horsepower motor. A sampling of Klein's colorful boxes and spinning tops are displayed in the foreground.

The lid of the cherry wood box shown at left is test-fitted while the workpiece is still mounted on the lathe. The lid is decorated with an ebony finial.

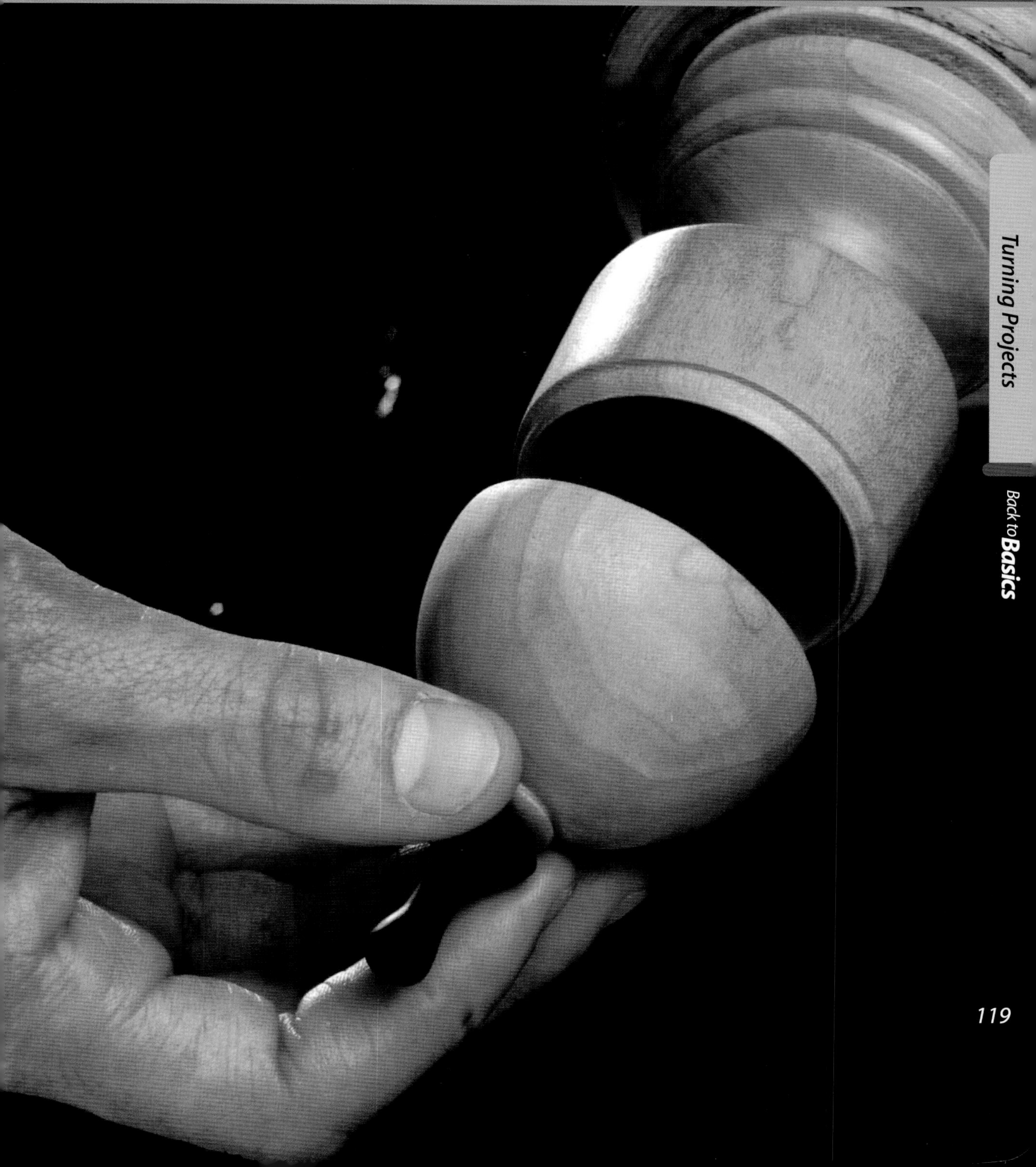

Off-Center Turning

By mounting a leg blank on the lathe off center, wood turners can create turnings such as the cabriole leg made from zebrawood shown above.

Turning a Cabriole Leg

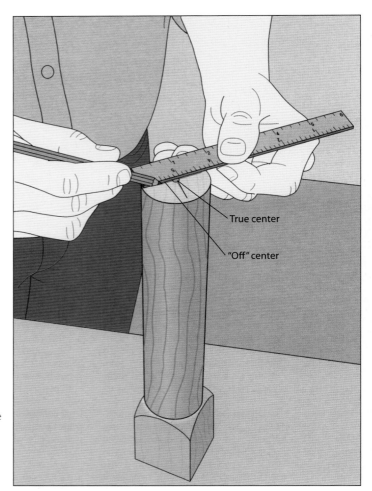

True center

"Off" center

Marking the "off" center

Mount your leg blank between true centers on the lathe, then use a skew chisel to make a shoulder cut on the piece *(page 62)*, defining the square section at the top of the leg. Next, turn the section below the shoulder to a cylinder with a roughing gouge *(page 55)*. Then, remove the workpiece from the lathe and mark a point on the bottom midway between the true center of the blank and the edge *(above)*. This off-center point will enable you to remount the leg on the lathe so you can produce its characteristic curve. Use an awl to make a small indentation on the pencil mark.

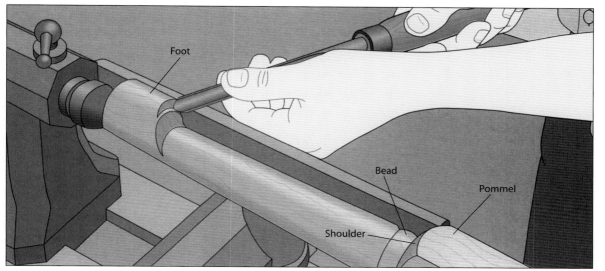

Foot

Bead

Pommel

Shoulder

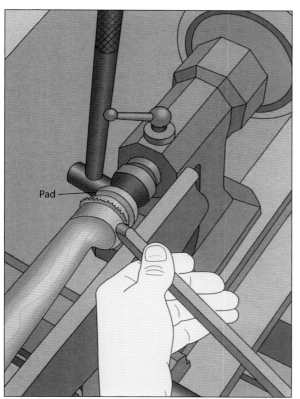

Pad

Turning the leg

Mount the top of the leg on center and the bottom on the off-center mark. Position the tool rest close to the blank, but not touching it, then turn on the lathe. The top of the blank will spin true, while the bottom will rotate eccentrically. Examine the blank as it spins. Note the solid core of stock along the center from the shoulder tapering down to the foot, surrounded by a lighter shadow—the off-center stock. Shape the cabriole leg by using a spindle gouge to remove the off-center stock down to the top of the foot. First, cut a gradual slope from the shoulder to the ankle of the leg, then shape a curved slope from the top of the foot to the ankle *(above)*. Make all your cuts downhill, with the flute of the gouge facing the direction of the cut. Brace the tool firmly on the tool rest, particularly when the bevel is not rubbing on the stock. Turn off the lathe periodically and check your progress. When you are satisfied with the shape of the leg, make any decorative cuts, such as turning a bead using a skew chisel *(page 69)*.

Turning the foot

Loosen the tailstock and reposition the live center on the true center of the bottom of the leg. Turn the foot to the shape you want using a spindle gouge and a skew chisel. Cabriole legs typically feature a round pad on the bottom of the foot. Adjust the tool rest for the cut and make a V-cut with a skew to separate the pad from the foot. Then shape the pad and foot, cutting downhill and keeping the bevel rubbing *(left)*.

121

Goblets

Goblets are usually decorative pieces turned to various shapes and sizes. They can be made surprisingly small, as shown in the photo at left.

Turning a Goblet

Hollowing the bowl section

Cut a blank for the goblet, mount it between centers, and prepare it for a glue block or a chuck. In this case, a three-way split ring chuck is used. Secure the blank in the chuck and mount the chuck on the lathe. Use a spindle gouge to turn the outside of the goblet to its maximum diameter, keeping the bevel rubbing and the flute facing the direction of the cut. Then, position the tool rest along the front of the blank so you can use the tip of a small bowl gouge to cut in the center of the workpiece following the inside of the goblet's bowl section. To begin this process, use a drill bit to bore a depth hole in the center of the bowl *(page 107)*. Then, use a bowl gouge or a round-nosed scraper to remove waste and thin the walls. With the gouge, point the bevel in the cutting direction and cut in along the sides of the hole to the center of the bowl, keeping the bevel rubbing and the flute pointing in the direction of the cut *(right)*. Because the gouge will be cutting across the grain, the cut may leave a slightly rough surface, depending on the type of wood you are using and the shape of the bowl. When the bowl is hollowed out, make a finishing cut from the center out using a round-nose side-cutting scraper *(page 127)*. Continue until you are satisfied with the shape of the interior.

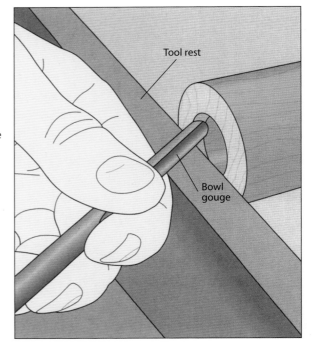

Tool rest

Bowl gouge

Sanding the inside of the bowl

Once you have hollowed the interior of the goblet, smooth the surface with progressively finer grits of sandpaper. Set the lathe to its lowest speed, fold the sheet in three plies, and hold the paper against the inside of the blank. Apply light pressure until the surface is smooth *(right)*.

Three-way
split ring chuck

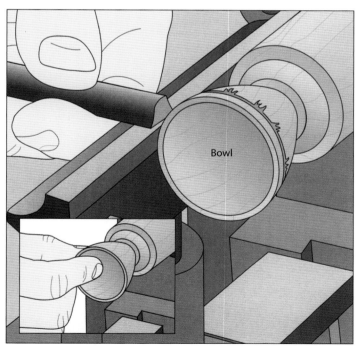

Bowl

Shaping the outside of the bowl

Once you have finished sanding the inside of the goblet, use a spindle gouge to shape the outside. Starting at the top of the bowl, cut downhill to the stem to shape the outside of the bowl to the desired diameter and curve *(left)*. Remember that the outside surface of the bowl should complement the inside. Aim for walls that are uniformly less than ⅛ inch thick. Cut gently, removing a small amount of stock with each pass to avoid cutting through the walls. Check the thickness periodically with your fingers *(inset)*. This will help you to develop a "feel" that is especially valuable for measuring small pieces, when working with calipers is difficult. Continue working the outside until the bowl assumes the desired shape, then sand its surface.

Rough-turning the stem

Starting about 1 inch from the headstock end of the bowl, begin turning the stem of the goblet to the desired diameter using a spindle gouge. Point the flute toward the bowl and keep the bevel rubbing while you make a sloping cut downward to the bottom of the bowl *(right)*. Continue in this manner until you have cut a portion of the stem to finished diameter. Then, slice off a bit more wood at the start of the cut and repeat the process on the next portion of the stem. Continue until the full length of the stem is rough-turned to the desired diameter.

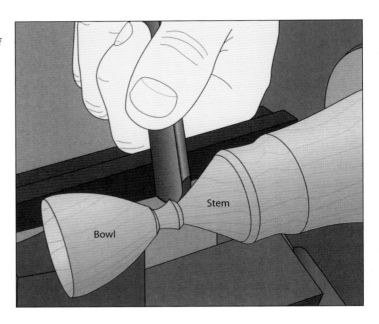

Stem

Bowl

Completing the stem

When you have turned the full length of the stem, turn the base, adding any decorative cuts, such as beads. For stability, the base should be at least equal in diameter to the bowl. Next, make finishing cuts on the stem. Because this portion is very thin, support the goblet during the cuts to prevent it from breaking. Bracing the heel of your hand against the tool rest, hold the bowl of the goblet lightly in your fingers. Gripping the gouge handle in your other hand, lay the blade on the tool rest and advance it carefully until the bevel is rubbing and the cutting edge is slicing into the stock. Starting at the base, point the flute in the direction of the cut, and make a light pass along the stem *(left)*, always cutting with the grain. Repeat light cuts as necessary to finish the stem.

Base

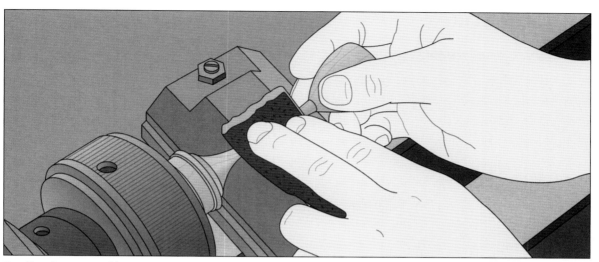

Sanding the stem and base

Move the tool rest out of way and fold a piece of sandpaper into a pad. Then, supporting the bowl with one hand, smooth the stem using progressively finer grits of paper *(above)*. Once the stem is sanded, smooth the base, and apply a finish *(page 110)*.

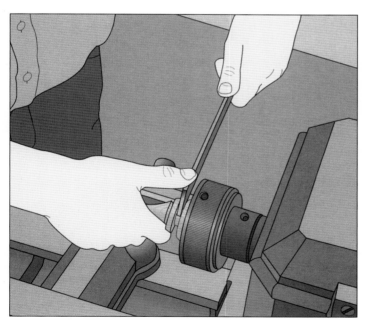

Parting off the goblet and undercutting the base

Once the goblet is finished, part it off just beneath the base. Support the goblet with one hand as you cut through the stock holding the parting tool in the other *(left)*. Cut until there is only a small bridge of wood holding the goblet to the waste wood. Then, turn off the lathe and use a handsaw to cut the goblet free. To ensure the base sits flat when the goblet is set down, sand the bottom by rubbing it across a piece of sandpaper taped to a work surface.

Turning Projects

Back to **Basics**

125

Lidded Boxes

Like goblets, lidded boxes can be made in many shapes and sizes, and with a variety of decorations. The cherry wood box shown on the near left is adorned with an ebony finial that is joined to the lid with a small round tenon. The box on the far left was turned from walnut.

Making a Lidded Box

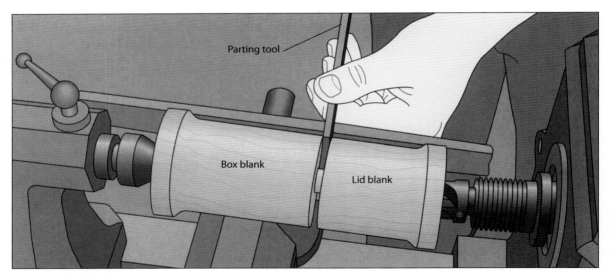

Parting tool

Box blank

Lid blank

Preparing the blank

Mount a blank longer than the desired height of the lidded box between centers and turn it to a cylinder. The piece will be split into blanks for the box and lid, as shown above, so they can be turned individually. If you will be using a collar chuck to remount the box and lid blanks to the lathe, turn the blank to a diameter of 2½ inches, with a flange of at least 2¾ inches at each end. These flanges will fit the collar chuck. Next, use a pencil to mark a line dividing the blank into its box and lid segments. Then cut the blank on the line with a parting tool *(above)*. Cut until only a small bridge of wood connects the two halves, then turn off the lathe, saw through the bridge, and remove the two blanks from the machine.

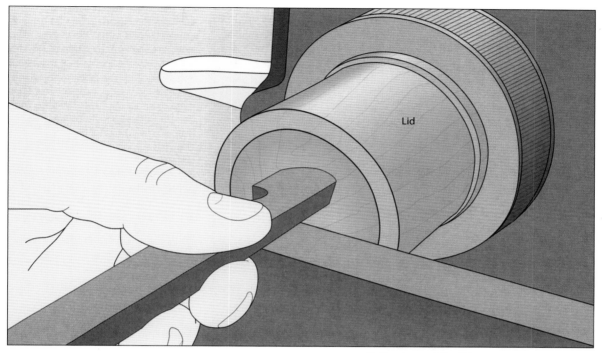

Shop Tip

A heat-free sanding pad
Hand-sanding on the lathe can
generate a lot of heat, which can
be transmitted to your fingers,
especially when sanding
the inside of boxes or
goblets. To insulate
your hands from
the heat, fold
your sandpaper
around a wad of
steel wool.

Hollowing out the lid

Use a chuck or glue block to mount the lid to
the headstock of the lathe *(page 97)*. In this case,
a collar chuck is being used. Hollow out the
lid of the box using a bowl gouge, a ring tool,
or a round-nosed side-cutting scraper. For the
scraper, position the tool rest close to the top of
the blank and high enough so the tool will cut
into the center of the stock. Align the scraper
with the center of the blank, raise the handle
slightly, and hold the blade flat on the tool
rest. Slowly push the tool into the blank; cut
from the center of the blank toward the rim
(above). Lower the handle slightly as you pull
the tool out of the lid. Continue cutting until
the inside of the lid has the desired shape and
smoothness. For a snug fit with the box, make
sure the walls at the rim are straight. Then sand
the interior *(page 123)* and finish it *(page 110)*.

Turning the outside of the lid

Turn the outside of the lid using a spindle gouge. Position the tool rest alongside the workpiece, then turn on the lathe and advance the tool so that it cuts into the stock. With the bevel rubbing and the flute facing the headstock, cut from large to small diameter to shape the lid. The outside should complement the inside; strive for walls of even thickness. Once the outside is turned, make any decorative cuts on the top of the lid. The example shown at left is decorated with a bead *(page 69)* cut with a skew chisel.

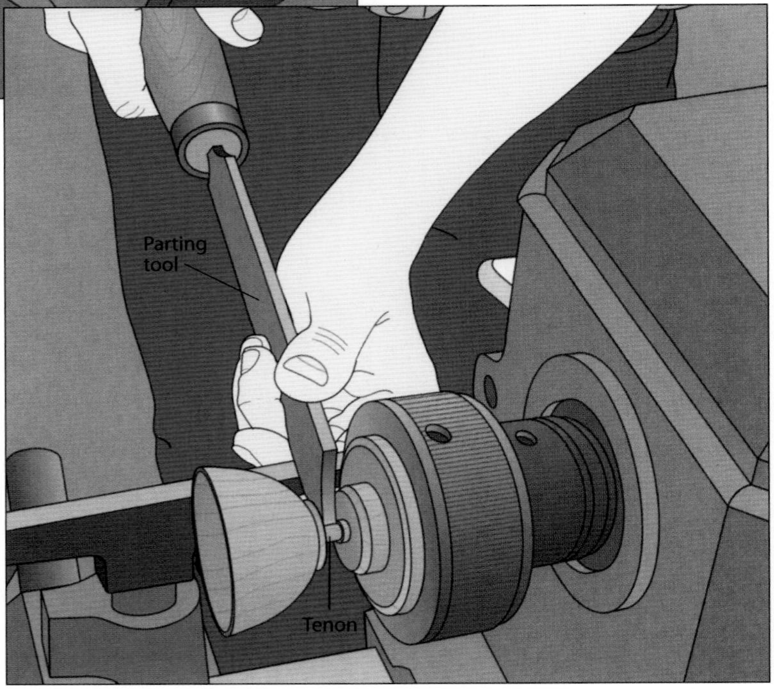

Skew chisel

Bead

Turning a tenon on the lid

Once its outside shape is turned, use a parting tool to cut a small round tenon on the top of the lid *(right)*. The tenon will be used to attach a finial to the lid; size the tenon to match the drill bit you will use to bore the mortise in the finial. Once the tenon is finished, sand the lid, using progressively finer grits of paper, and apply a finish *(page 110)*. Use a handsaw to cut the piece off the lathe.

Parting tool

Tenon

Fitting the lid on the box

Cut a blank for the finial, using a wood that contrasts with the species used for the lid. Bore a hole in the finial blank to fit the tenon on the lid, then join the two pieces with cyanoacrylate glue. Next, mount the box in a collar chuck. Using a parting tool, carefully turn a rabbet around the rim to accommodate the lid. The rabbet cheek must be straight and perpendicular to the rabbet shoulder to fit the lid properly. Test-fit the lid frequently *(right)* as you turn the rabbet until the fit is snug.

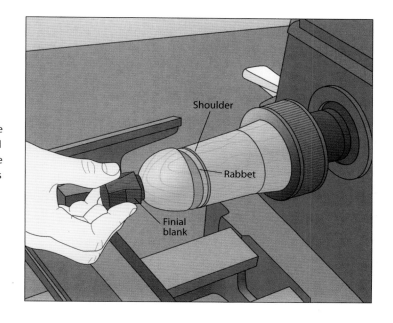

Shoulder

Rabbet

Finial blank

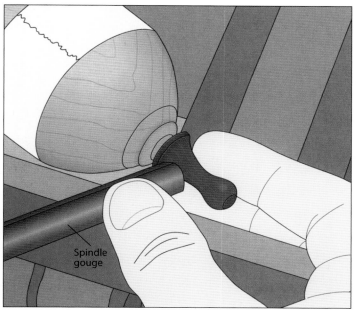

Spindle gouge

Turning the finial

Tape the lid securely to the box to turn the finial. Position the tool rest alongside the lid and finial. Supporting the finial lightly with one hand, set the blade on the tool rest and advance it until it cuts into the stock. Shape the finial as desired, cutting downhill with the bevel rubbing throughout the cut *(left)*. Sand and finish the tip of the lid, then remove it from the box.

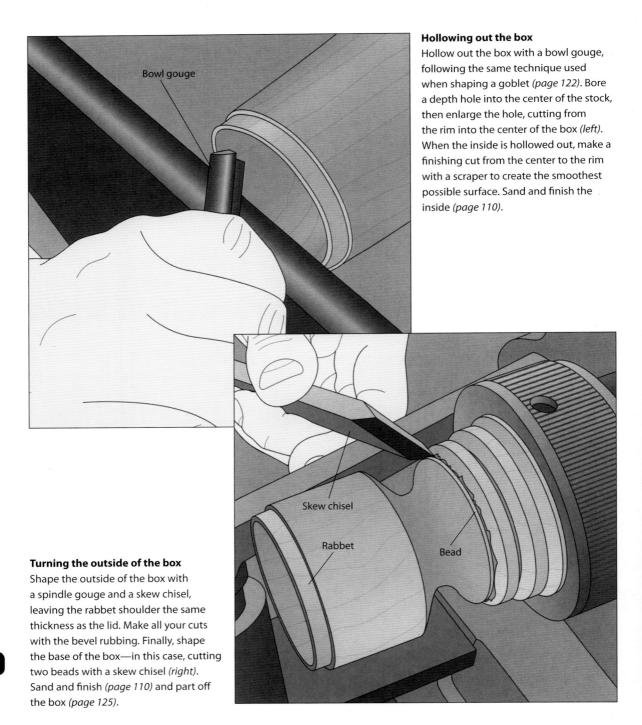

Bowl gouge

Skew chisel

Rabbet

Bead

Hollowing out the box

Hollow out the box with a bowl gouge, following the same technique used when shaping a goblet *(page 122)*. Bore a depth hole into the center of the stock, then enlarge the hole, cutting from the rim into the center of the box *(left)*. When the inside is hollowed out, make a finishing cut from the center to the rim with a scraper to create the smoothest possible surface. Sand and finish the inside *(page 110)*.

Turning the outside of the box

Shape the outside of the box with a spindle gouge and a skew chisel, leaving the rabbet shoulder the same thickness as the lid. Make all your cuts with the bevel rubbing. Finally, shape the base of the box—in this case, cutting two beads with a skew chisel *(right)*. Sand and finish *(page 110)* and part off the box *(page 125)*.

Dried Flower Vase

Dried flower vases, sometimes called weed pots, can be turned from off-cuts and scraps that would normally be consigned to firewood. And, so long as they are used to hold dried or artificial flowers or grasses, no finish or sealer is needed inside. The examples shown in the photo above illustrate sample designs. The vessel on the left was fashioned from a hickory branch. The bark was left on at the base to impart a rustic flavor. Steps for turning this vase are presented at right and on the following pages.

Making a Dried Flower Vase

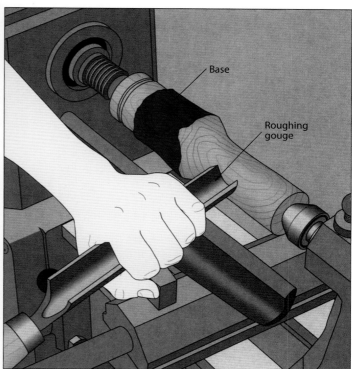

Base

Roughing gouge

Roughing the outside

Mount the blank between centers on your lathe. The blank shown above is from a partly dry hickory branch that has a small knot near the bottom. This involves two design considerations. First, the bark will be left on the base of the finished piece. Second, the wood may warp or crack as it dries. Mount the blank between centers and turn the straight portion of the piece to fit a chuck—in this case, a three-way split ring chuck *(page 95)*, leaving the bark on at the base. Hold a roughing gouge on the tool rest and move it along the blank to make the cut *(above)*, keeping the bevel rubbing throughout the operation. When the top of the blank is turned to shape, mount it on the chuck and hollow out the piece. A vase for dried flowers does not need to have a clean inside surface, so simply install a Jacobs chuck in the tailstock and fit it with a wood bit. Set the lathe to its slowest speed, turn on the machine, and advance the tailstock to bore the hole. Once the inside is hollowed out, shape the mouth with a bowl gouge, then finish turning and decorate the outside.

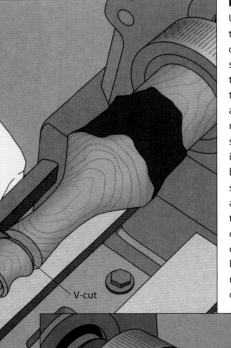

Skew chisel

V-cut

Finish turning

Use a spindle gouge to smooth the transition between the base and neck of the vessel, cutting downhill until a smooth curve joins the two sections of the piece. Next, decorate the outside of the vase as desired. For this model, use a skew chisel to make a V-cut below the mouth *(left)*. Pivot the blade into the stock, raising the handle until the cut is the required depth. Then rotate the blade to either side to cut away both sides of the groove to form a V. Now use a spindle gouge to turn a cove joining the V-cut to the mouth. Chamfer the rim of the mouth, then make a smoothing cut with the spindle gouge down the length of the pot, keeping the bevel rubbing and the flute pointed in the direction of the cut.

Sanding

Once you have shaped the vase, move the tool rest out of the way and start to smooth the piece with 220-grit sandpaper. Use progressively finer grits until you attain the finish you want. Reduce the lathe to its slowest speed, fold the paper twice, and hold it against the spinning blank. For the best possible control, hold the paper below the center axis of the lathe. When you are finished sanding, apply a finish *(page 110)*, if desired. Part the piece off the chuck and clean up the bottom *(page 125)*.

An Alternative Dried Flower Vase

Inserting wood pegs

Pegs cut from a contrasting wood provide an easy way to add a design detail to a turning. Once cut, they are inserted in holes drilled in the vessel and then turned flush when the vase is remounted on the lathe for finish turning. Begin by mounting a blank between centers and turning it to a cylinder. Then use a parting tool to prepare the piece for mounting on the lathe—in this case, a three-way split ring chuck *(page 95)*—turning a groove for the rings at the headstock end of the piece. Once the groove is cut, switch to a spindle gouge to rough-turn the pot to the desired shape. Now turn off the lathe and mark the location of the wood pegs. These may be randomly placed or put in a pattern. Use a plug cutter on a drill press to cut the pegs. Then bore holes in your workpiece for the pegs. Use a V-block to hold the pot for the cuts. Finally, spread some glue in the holes and insert the pegs *(right)*. Allow the glue to cure before finish-turning the piece.

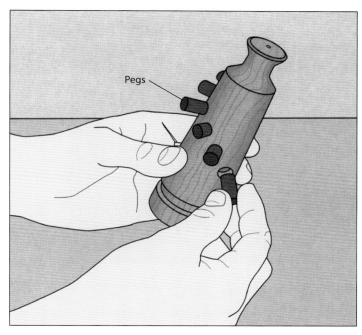

Pegs

Finish-turning the vase

Chuck the pot to the headstock of the lathe using the three-way split ring chuck. Reduce the lathe speed to its lowest setting and use a Jacobs chuck and spade bit to hollow out the work. Now, finish-turn the piece with a spindle gouge, bringing the pegs flush with the outside and making light smoothing cuts along the outside until you are satisfied with the finish. Finally, adjust the tool rest to the front of the piece and chamfer the edge of the mouth using a bowl gouge *(left)*. Sand and finish the piece as desired, then part it off the from the chuck and clean up the bottom *(page 125)*.

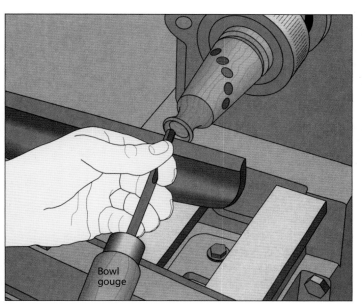

Bowl gouge

Tabletops

The outboard spindle on the Wadkin Bursgreen lathe shown in the photo at left provides sufficient swing to accommodate large turnings, like this round mahogany tabletop, designed for a small pedestal table or a candlestand.

Turning a Tabletop

Shaping the underside

Use a band saw to cut your blank into a circle slightly larger than the finished diameter of the tabletop. Turn the underside first, as shown at right, then shape the top surface. Fasten a glue block *(page 87)* to each side of the blank and a faceplate to one of the blocks, and screw the faceplate on the outboard spindle of the lathe. Position the tool rest at a 45° angle to the corner of the blank and true the circumference with a bowl or spindle gouge. To chamfer the circumference, roll the gouge so the right-hand side of the blade is on the tool rest with the flute pointing up at a 45° angle in the direction of the cut. Starting on the bottom of the tabletop about ½ inch from the corner of the blank, advance the tool until the bevel rubs on the stock. Raise the tool handle until the edge is cutting, then move the tool to the right to chamfer the corner *(right)*. Repeat the cut, rounding the corner until you are satisfied with its shape. Smooth the underside with a flat scraper, then make a cut on the circumference of the outside glue block to be sure it is perfectly centered on the piece. Sand the surface, turn off the lathe, and mark a series of concentric rings on the glue block to help center it on the faceplate when you reverse the piece for the next step.

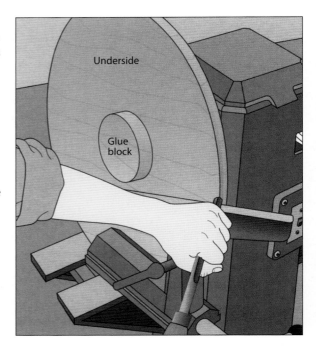

Underside

Glue block

Shaping the rim

Remove the faceplate from the workpiece, then reattach it to the bottom glue block, centering the block with the rings you marked. Screw the faceplate to the outboard spindle and turn on the lathe. Use a gouge to cut away the glue block on the top, then make a light cut across the top to true the surface. Now define the rim. In this example, most of the surface will be recessed, leaving a raised rim. Starting about ½ inch from the circumference of the blank, begin cutting a recess from right to left, working towards the center of the top. This cut runs partially across the grain. To make the cutting a bit easier, rotate the gouge once you have extended the recess partway across the top so the flute faces the right-hand edge of the blank. Cut into the waste from the other side, biting off about ¼ inch of stock with each cut *(right)*. Continue in this manner until you have removed most of the waste and the recess is about ½ inch deep.

Raised rim

Top surface

Gouge

Flat scraper

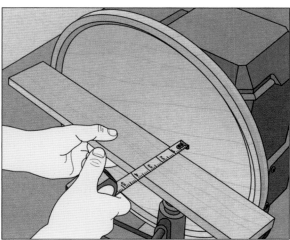

Flattening the recess

Use a flat scraper to smooth the surface of the tabletop. Starting at the center of the top, set the scraper blade flat on the tool rest. Pivot the handle up and advance the tool until the burr is cutting the wood. Keeping the edge of the scraper square to the top, move the tool to the right, removing a small amount of stock and trying to keep the surface even *(above, left)*. Continue until the cut meets the raised rim you defined before. To check the depth of cut as you go, hold a straightedge across the middle of the workpiece, making sure to contact the rim at two points. Use a tape measure to check the gap between the edge and the tabletop at several points *(above, right)*. Continue cutting until the depth of the recess is uniform all across the top. Then use a gouge to clean up the transition between the rim and the recess, if necessary. Sand and finish the top *(page 110)*, then remove the piece from the lathe and use a saw or chisel to remove the glue block. Sand away any traces of the block and finish the underside of the top.

135

Laminated Bowls

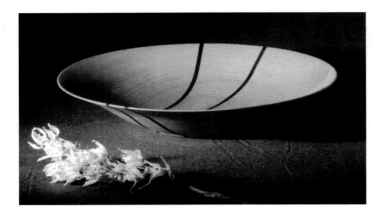

Popularized by wood turner Dale Nish, the technique of adding contrasting wood veneers to bowls can be used to create a unique design. The laminated bowl shown in the photo at left was turned from cherry and two strips of shop-made pau ferro veneer.

Turning a Laminated Bowl

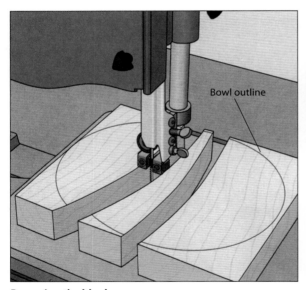

Bowl outline

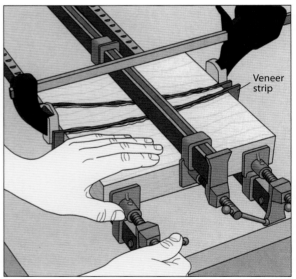

Veneer strip

Preparing the blank

Outline the bowl on your blank and mark the location of the veneer strips; the lines should run roughly parallel to the grain of the blank. Band saw along the lines, separating the blank into three pieces *(above, left)*. Sand the cut edges to remove any ridges left by the saw blade. Now, prepare two lengths of commercial or shop-made veneer slightly longer than the cuts. Spread a thin coat of glue on both sides of the veneer and on the cut edges of the blank. Then, reassemble and clamp the blank with the veneer strips in the kerfs. Use as many clamps as necessary to apply even pressure. Because the kerfs are curved, it may be necessary to apply an additional clamp perpendicular to the others to keep the pieces from sliding out of alignment *(above, right)*.

Turning the bottom

Once the glue has cured, cut the blank into a circle along the marked outline on the band saw. Next, use a faceplate *(page 86)* to mount the blank on the lathe's headstock spindle. Start by preparing the base for mounting so you can hollow out the inside of the bowl. In this case, a dovetailed recess for a scroll chuck was cut in the base with a side-cutting skew scraper *(page 103)*. Then shape the bottom of the bowl using standard bowl-turning techniques, first rounding the corner of the blank, and then shaping the outside walls *(page 100)*. Cut from the bottom toward the top of the bowl, keeping the bevel rubbing and the flute pointed in the direction of the cut *(right)*. When you are satisfied with the shape of the outside, sand and finish the surface.

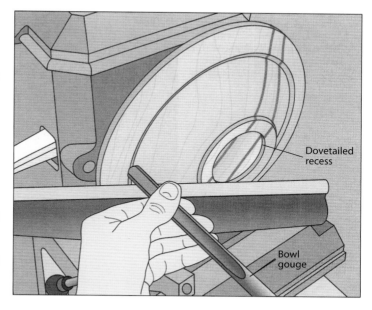

Dovetailed
recess

Bowl
gouge

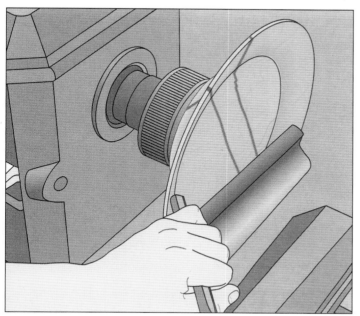

Hollowing out the bowl

Reverse the bowl and mount it on the lathe with a scroll chuck. Position the tool rest parallel to the rim and begin hollowing out the bowl with a bowl gouge, starting just to the left of center and cutting in to the center. Move the gouge slightly to the left and cut in again. Gradually work your way out to the rim, removing most of the waste and making sure that each cut is made from left to right. Finish shaping the bowl cutting from the rim to the center *(left)*. Once the bowl is hollowed out, it can be shear scraped, if necessary, sanded, and finished.

Laminated Plates

The laminated plate shown in the photo at left was made with purple-heart and a pau amarello insert bordered by two strips of zebrawood. The technique for turning such a piece is presented below and on the next page.

Turning a Laminated Plate

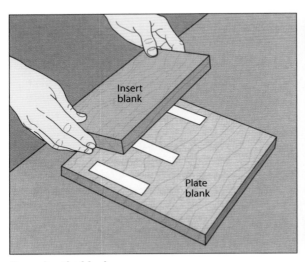

Insert blank

Plate blank

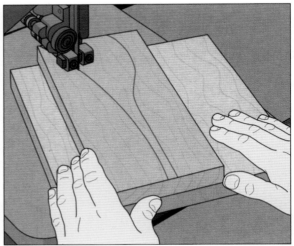

Preparing the blank

Cut two 1-inch-thick blanks: one for the main part of the plate and a narrower piece of contrasting stock for the insert. Apply a few strips of double-sided tape to the plate blank over the area where the insert will be located and fasten the insert in place *(above, left)*; make sure the edges and ends of the blanks are aligned. Outline the final shape of the insert on the board's top face with a pencil. Cut along the lines on the band saw, cutting through both boards *(above, right)*. Sand the cut edges to eliminate any ridges left by the saw blade.

Assembling the blank

Pry the insert off the blank and discard the waste pieces. Prepare two strips of commercial or shop-made veneer as wide as the thickness of the blanks and at least as long. Assemble the blank on a work surface, placing the veneer strips alongside the insert and then adding the two outside cuts from the plate blank. Glue and clamp the pieces together. Once the adhesive has cured, trim the ends of the veneer flush with the edges of the blanks, then cut a circle out of the assembly the diameter of the finished plate on the band saw.

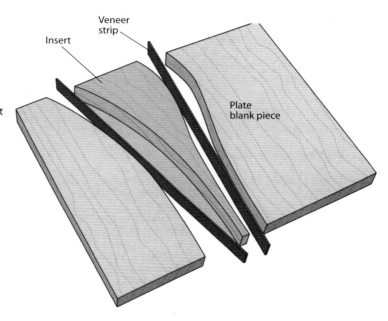

Insert

Veneer strip

Plate blank piece

Turning the plate

Secure the plate on the lathe using the faceplate with a glue block or double-sided tape *(page 87)*. Turn the bottom of the plate first, cutting from the center to the rim, then flatten the bottom with a square-end scraper. Next, prepare the base so the piece can be reversed and chucked to hollow out the inside. Using a bowl gouge, turn the inside, moving from the rim to the center *(left)*. Sand and finish the piece, then reverse it to finish shaping the bottom, using a commercial scroll chuck with rubber posts. *(page 112)*.

Bowl gouge

Glossary

A-B-C

Baluster: A vertical post that runs between the handrail and the treads of a staircase; may be turned, carved, or chamfered.

Bead: A convex shape turned in spindle work; *See cove.*

Bevel: The sloping surface at the tip of a turning tool's blade.

Billet: A short length of wood.

Blank: A length or block of wood used for turning.

Burnishing: The last step in sharpening a scraper blade, usually performed with a metal rod called a burnisher; forms a burr on the blade.

Burr: A small ridge created on the flat face of turning tool blades as a result of sharpening or burnishing.

Cabriole leg: A type of furniture leg characterized by rounded contours designed to imitate the graceful leg of a leaping animal.

Chuck: An accessory mounted in the headstock or tailstock of a lathe to hold a blank for turning.

Collet chuck: A chuck or turning accessory with contracting or expanding jaws to hold work for faceplate turning.

Combination chuck: A multipurpose chuck with interlocking parts that enable it to be used as any of several different types of chuck.

Concave: A rounded, depressed shape, such as the inside of a bowl.

Convex: A rounded, raised shape, such as the outside of a bowl.

Cove: A concave detail turned in spindle work. *See bead.*

Cutting tool: Any turning tool used to shape workpieces in turning; includes skew chisels, roughing gouges, bowl gouges, and spindle gouges. *See scraping tool.*

D-E-F-G-H-I

Dead center: A fixed center mounted in the tailstock of a lathe to support spindle work. *See live center.*

Dovetail: A shape that is formed to join a blank for faceplate turning to a chuck by means of a tapered recess in the blank that mates with the expanding or contracting jaws of the chuck.

Downhill cutting: In spindle work, cutting with the grain rather than against it; working from a high point to a low point.

Drive center: A two-or four-pronged center mounted in the headstock of a lathe to secure a workpiece for spindle turning.

End grain: The ends of the wood fibers in a workpiece.

Faceplate turning: A turning technique in which the grain of the workpiece is perpendicular to the lathe's axis; the workpiece is usually only mounted to the headstock of the machine. *See spindle turning.*

Fillet: A flat section on a spindle turning between rounded elements.

Fingernail grind: The curved shape ground on the edge of a turning gouge; so-called because the profile is similar to the curve on the end of a fingernail.

Finial: A turned or carved ornament that adorns the top of a bedpost, stair baluster, turned box, or a piece of furniture.

Flute: Concave channels, usually evenly spaced, carved along the length of spindle turnings such as chair legs and balusters. *See reed.* Also, the curve in the blade of a tool.

Grain: The arrangement and direction of the fibers that make up wood.

Green wood: Wood that has not been dried.

Grit: The density and size of abrasive particles on a piece of sandpaper or a grinding wheel.

Headstock: The fixed end of a lathe incorporating the drive spindle; connected to the motor by one or more drive belts. *See tailstock.*

Hollow grind: A slightly concave bevel ground on the cutting edge of a turning tool by a grinding wheel.

Indexing head: An accessory on some lathes that enables the headstock to be rotated manually by equal increments.

J-K-L-M-N-O-P-Q

Jig: A device for guiding a tool or holding a workpiece in position.

Kickback: The tendency of a cutting tool to be thrown back in the direction of the operator.

Lathe capacity: The distance between centers on a lathe as well as twice the distance between headstock spindle and lathe bed; limits the length of spindle work that can be mounted on the machine. *See swing.*

Live center: A ball-bearing center mounted in the tailstock of a lathe to support spindle work; bearings allow center to spin with the work. *See dead center.*

Morse taper: A tapered shaft on lathe centers and chucks that matches a reverse taper in the headstock or tailstock, holding the center or chuck in place with a friction fit.

Parting off: Cutting a turning to length on the lathe with a parting tool or skew chisel and removing it while the machine is still running.

Parting tool: A cutting tool used to make sizing cuts and part off workpieces.

Peeling cut: A roughing-out technique in spindle work that uses the heel of a skew chisel to remove stock quickly.

Planing cut: A final smoothing cut with a skew chisel in spindle work designed to create a surface that needs little sanding.

Pole lathe: An early version of the lathe powered by a treadle attached to a pole or tree sapling by means of a cord.

Pommel: A rounded shoulder produced in spindle work; serves to separate square and cylindrical sections of a workpiece.

Pumice: A volcanic rock that is ground to a powdery consistency for use as an abrasive.

R-S

Radiused skew: A skew chisel featuring a curved cutting edge rather than a straight one; helps avoid contact with points.

Reed: An evenly spaced, convex embellishment carved along the length of spindle turnings such as chair legs and balusters. *See flute.*

Reverse-profile template: A shop-made template made of wood or plastic shaped to the desired profile of a turning; used to turn multiple copies of the same shape.

Scraping tool: A turning tool that removes stock with a burr; used to shape bowls, plates, and other faceplate work. *See cutting tool.*

Shear scraping: A turning technique in which a scraper is used with its edge at approximately 45° to the blank; the burr of the scraper is drawn lightly across the work to produce a smooth surface.

Sizing cut: A cut with a parting tool to a specific depth.

Skew chisel: A cutting tool with an angled cutting edge beveled on both sides; used to make basic and decorative spindle cuts.

Spindle turning: A turning technique in which the grain of the workpiece is parallel to the lathe's axis; the workpiece is held between centers in the tailstock and headstock. Also known as turning between centers. *See faceplate turning.*

Split turning: A turning technique in which a blank is cut into halves or quarters, then glued back together and turned; the finished turning is then easy to pry apart.

Steady rest: A lathe accessory that slides along the lathe bed to hold a long workpiece steady.

Swing: Twice the distance between the headstock spindle and lathe bed.

T-U-V-W-X-Y-Z

Tailstock: The adjustable end of a lathe that slides along the lathe bed and incorporates the tailstock spindle. *See headstock.*

Taper: A sloping cut on a spindle turning that decreases its thickness at one end.

Tearout: The tendency of a blade to tear the fibers of the wood, rather than cutting them cleanly, leaving ragged edges on the workpiece.

Tool rest: An adjustable stand that slides along the lathe bed, providing a fulcrum point for a turning tool.

Urn: A decorative element turned in spindle work; often part of a finial.

Veneer: A thin layer of decorative wood used to dress up a more common species of wood.

Wheel dresser: A device used to true the working surface of a grinding wheel and expose fresh abrasive.

Index

Back to **Basics**   *Straight Talk for Today's **Woodworker***

Get *Back to Basics* with the core information you need to succeed. This new series offers a clear road map of fundamental woodworking knowledge on sixteen essential topics. It explains what's important to know now and what can be left for later. Best of all, it's presented in the plain-spoken language you'd like to hear from a trusted friend or relative. The world's already complicated—your woodworking information shouldn't be.

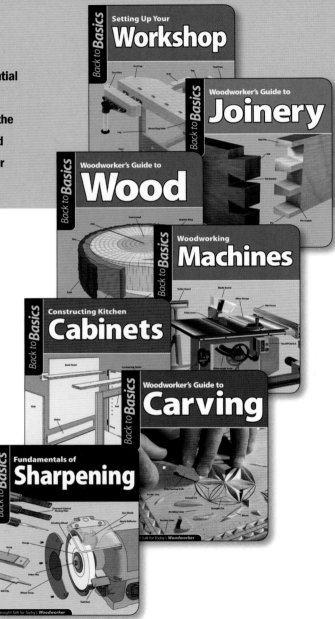

Setting Up Your Workshop

ISBN: 978-1-56523-463-5
$19.95 • 152 Pages

Woodworker's Guide to Joinery

ISBN: 978-1-56523-462-8
$19.95 • 192 Pages

Woodworker's Guide to Wood

ISBN: 978-1-56523-464-2
$19.95 • 160 Pages

Woodworking Machines

ISBN: 978-1-56523-465-9
$19.95 • 192 Pages

Constructing Kitchen Cabinets

ISBN: 978-1-56523-466-6
$19.95 • 144 Pages

Woodworker's Guide to Carving

ISBN: 978-1-56523-497-0
$19.95 • 160 Pages

Fundamentals of Sharpening

ISBN: 978-1-56523-496-3
$19.95 • 120 Pages